Unfailing Love

God's Answer to a Troubled Family

You are such a blessing
May you always
know God's love.

Carol Genengels

Carol Genengels

PRESS

Unfailing Love
by Carol Genengels

Printed in the United States of America

ISBN 1-594671-40-0

www.xulonpress.com

Foreword

*E*ven if you do not have a chronically ill daughter, a totally difficult foster child or a dysfunctional family of origin, you are going to love this book.

Even if you do not have teenagers living less than honorably, even if your faith in God is only tentative, even if your heart and your dreams are not broken, you are going to love this book.

If you have ever doubted that you could be a leader, that you could be friends with those who treat you cruelly, or that your life could ever count for something good, you are going to love this book.

This past June, I sat in my backyard and read Carol Genengels' manuscript. My husband, Bill, gruffly asked, "What are you doing?"

"I'm reading a story for a friend."

He frowned, "I thought you were taking the summer off from work."

"Trust me, Bill, this is not work. This is a joy. I love this book."

The reason I love it, and you will too, is that

Carol has chosen to be honest to the point of being transparent. You will walk beside her on a road strewn with crises, rejections and tears. You will be there as the road widens into faith and hope. You will thank God that Carol wrote her story so that you could travel with her.

When you come to the end, you may even invite Jesus to walk as intimately with you as He walks with her.

Pat King

AND
Ted, Gigi, Shawn, & Ryan
*You've taught me so much about love
To my prayer partners **Jane and Ann** —
what a ride it's been!*

Special Thanks To 'Ginny'
Your prayers launched this project

*A million thanks to everyone who gave feedback
regarding the manuscript. I couldn't have done it
without you. To God be the Glory.*

*Many of the names in this book have been changed
to protect the privacy of the individuals involved.

Unfailing Love

Prologue

"O Love that will not let me go,
I rest my weary soul in Thee,
I give Thee back the life I owe,
that in Thine ocean depths
its flow may richer, fuller be.
O Joy that seeketh me thro' pain,
I cannot close my heart to Thee.
I trace the rainbow thro' the rain,
and feel the promise is not vain,
that morn shall tearless be."
Song text—*O Love That Wilt Not Let Me Go*:
by George Matheson

Your love, O Lord, reaches to the heavens, your
faithfulness to the skies... How priceless is your
unfailing love! Both high and low among men
find refuge in the shadow of your wings
Psalm 36:5&7 (NIV).

Would the creator of the universe really pour His unfailing love on my troubled family? How could He possibly single out my heart's cry from the six billion people inhabiting this planet?

Contents

Chapter One

Seeds of Faith

Seattle, Washington
Children's Hospital — 1973

*A*utomatic double doors closed behind me as I entered the world of sick children. I felt my stomach churning—a sinking nauseous feeling. Hospitals unnerved me with their antiseptic odors and mysterious corridors. My twelve year old daughter, Gigi, was waiting for me upstairs. I bypassed a crowded lobby where anxious relatives awaited news of their loved ones. Like most mothers of hospitalized children, I sought hope around every gleaming corner. I paused by a room where a tiny boy lay sleeping in a crib. An anguished young father grieved at his bedside. Guilt and despair seemed to be his only companions; it had been an accident with his gun, a stray bullet. Now he helplessly watched machines and pulsing wires keep his son alive.

I continued on down the hall, and entered a room with four beds. Two of them were unoccupied. Gigi was standing near the bed of a girl with a huge, misshapen head.

"Hi there!" I said in my cheeriest voice. Gigi turned and ran into my arms. "Mama!"

I stroked her straight blonde hair as she clung to me. "What are you doing out of bed?" I playfully scolded

"I was helping Mandy with her lunch."

Gigi dutifully crossed the room and climbed onto her mechanical bed. She whispered in my ear, "Mama, that poor girl has water on her brain!"

I tried not to stare at the child's distorted features. Instead, I focused on Gigi's beautiful amber eyes. Deep bluish shadows beneath them gave subtle clues to the battle raging within her gangly body. I tucked the thin cotton blanket around her torso—mostly arms and legs.

"When can we go home?" she asked. Before I could answer a woman rushed into the room and began washing her hands at the sink. "Oh Good, you're here," she said. She dried her hands on a paper towel and reached for Gigi's chart. "You are her mother aren't you?"

"Yes."

"I'm Dr. *Lee," she said crisply as she leafed through the chart. Her starched white jacket accentuated her serious dark eyes and black hair. "Hmmm.....we just can't seem to pinpoint the cause of her fevers." She shrugged and sighed, "I guess you'll just have to learn to live with it, that's all."

"But—we have lived with it, ever since she was a toddler."

"Look, I'm really sorry, but if the doctors here at Children's can't find a diagnosis, I seriously doubt anyone could! Unless we do painful bone marrow tests there's not much more we can do. Is that what you want?"

"Well, no... of course not. I don't know *what* to do anymore."

"Talk to your pediatrician, see if he wants to pursue this further. In the meantime, I'll forward the test results to him. You can take your daughter home now."

She scribbled in the chart, glanced at her watch, and dashed from the room. I wanted to chase her down the hall and drag her back: *You've got to have some answers, after all these tests.*

Gigi's questioning eyes sought mine. I tried to hide my disappointment, "Look's like you're going home, honey."

I placed a long distance phone call to our pediatrician in Bremerton. His soothing voice reassured me, "Don't lose heart, we'll continue to keep a close eye on her."

Dr. H. was puzzled by the chronic malady that began with a raw sore throat and fatigue. Gigi's throat pain usually intensified while her temperature soared as high as 105-106 degrees. Hallucinations and nightmares often accompanied the raging fevers, along with chills, nausea and vomiting. The symptoms lasted about a week before they subsided. Three or four weeks later the cycle began all over again.

Gigi's doctor asked if we'd been in the tropics—because her mottled skin resembled malaria patients. We'd never visited the tropics. He suspected an auto immune deficiency disease.

I learned to take throat cultures at home to transport to the lab. The cultures always proved to be viral, never strep. Our chaotic lives included disrupted vacations, canceled sleep-overs, and postponed parties. A small fortune was spent on antibiotics and doctor bills. Days were swallowed up driving to appointments, sitting in waiting rooms, and awaiting lab results.

A nurse brought Gigi's clothing in a plastic bag. "You're free to go now dear," she said. I untied the back of my daughter's hospital gown where shoulder blades protruded like budding wings. Her skinny arms and hips bore purple bruises from being poked and prodded. She was more than ready to leave the doctors and needles behind.

Gigi dressed in denim pants and a sweater before bidding her roommate good-bye. The nurse pushed her in a wheelchair as we headed for the cashier's office. I signed insurance papers and pondered, *now what?*

A cloud of discouragement hovered overhead as we left the hospital. I hungrily gulped a deep breath of fresh air. My friend, Nancy, was waiting for us with my baby Ryan. He reached for his sister and Gigi took him in her arms.

"You don't look very happy," Nancy said.

"What'd the doctor say anyway?"

"Learn to live with it." I muttered with a tinge of sarcasm.

Nancy unlocked the car doors and the children settled in the back seat. I joined her in the front seat. She started the engine and merged into traffic. While we waited at a traffic light, Nancy faced me. "Pastor Rienschie thinks there might be something to this faith healing stuff that's happening in some churches."

"Faith healing?"

We'd been members of Pastor Rienschie's Church before we moved away. I'd never heard him talk that way before. As Nancy brought me up-to-date on the pastor's latest insights, a seedling of hope lodged in the parched soil of my heart. I pondered her words long after we returned to our home in Seabeck, Washington on Hood Canal.

I didn't really believe faith healing applied much these days. Though I attended church faithfully with my husband and children, I felt numb spiritually. I sang hymns out of habit and daydreamed during sermons. But secretly, I longed to hear something that might change my life.

Ted would usually nod off during sermons and I'd elbow him every few minutes to keep him awake. After church we'd enjoy coffee and doughnuts in the fellowship hall and visit with friends. On our way home we'd quiz the kids about Sunday School. They usually had good reports. But one Sunday we couldn't help but laugh at Gigi's ten year old brother, Shawn's, report. He had a teacher who worked for the Coca Cola company. That afternoon, Shawn excitedly shared what he'd learned in class. "Hi-C is made by the Coke company!"

At times, things looked almost hopeless. Ted was preoccupied with his career, we quarreled a lot, and Gigi was usually sick. God seemed far away as I battled bouts of depression.

* * * *

Our assistant pastor preached a fiery sermon one Sunday morning. "Strange things are happening in the Church today. Some people claim supernatural gifts of healing or speaking in tongues." He became agitated as he expressed his alarm over the charismatic movement, and the potential harm posed to believers. He was very convincing.

After church I lingered in the library amongst a vast array of books. *What am I looking for? Why do I feel such a void?* I silently prayed a deep, desperate plea: *Please God, help me to grow spiritually or let me die spiritually, I just can't stand the place I'm in any longer!*

Our senior pastor's wife, Katie, entered the library. I asked her to recommend a good book. The titles she pointed out seemed as dry and lifeless as I felt.

"How's your family doing?" she asked.

"Oh, Gigi was sick again." I said. Katie listened as I told her my story.

"Why don't you call the women's prayer group?" She suggested.

"Prayer group?"

"They meet every week. Honestly, they've had some remarkable answers to prayer. Here, let me give you the leader's name and number." Katie wrote on a slip of paper and handed it to me. I stuffed the note in my purse as I left the library.

Answered Prayer? Prayer was my last resort; the doctors couldn't help. *Could God?*

The next morning, after the kids left for school, I toyed with the notion of calling the lady from the prayer group. Gigi was so far behind in school that her grades were suffering. I put on a fresh pot of coffee and loaded the dishwasher. I got my purse and rummaged for the phone number. I placed the note on the counter and poured a cup of coffee—savoring the rich aroma. My thoughts swirled like the cream I stirred in the mug. *Do I really want to do this?*

I decided to dial the number before I lost my nerve. A woman answered after a few rings. "Hello."

"Hi...ah...my name is Carol Genengels ... from Our Saviour's. Is this Phyllis?"

"Yes." She said.

"The reason I called is... er, Katie Nesse gave me your number. I understand you belong to a prayer group?"

"Yes."

I explained Gigi's problem and the hopeless prognosis. "Do you think your group could—maybe pray for her?"

"Certainly!" She said. "Would you like us to come to your home to pray for Gigi? We could anoint her with oil, like we're instructed to do in the Bible."

"Anoint with oil? Well ... ah ... I don't know." (It didn't sound very Lutheran to me.)

"Think about it! The Word instructs us to call for the elders of the church to pray and lay hands on the sick. Read James, chapter 5, in the Bible. In the meantime we'll pray for Gigi, but please don't hesitate to call again if you want us to come and pray with her."

"Okay. Thanks, thanks a lot."

"You're very welcome."

Anoint with oil? Lay hands? That was okay for Bible days maybe, but not now. I recalled Nancy's words: *There might be something to this faith healing stuff....*

I decided to give Pastor Nesse a call. His booming sermons kept everyone awake, even Ted! He asked me to meet him at the church.

I sat in front of the huge desk of my pastor, Milton Nesse, an avid fisherman and ex-football player. A framed picture of his wife and five children stood out amongst books and papers. I questioned him about Phyllis, the prayer group, and "praying with oil."

He told me about a teenage girl in the congregation. She'd been seriously ill with leukemia, and the doctors hadn't offered much hope. Pastor Nesse and the prayer group went to the hospital, anointed her with oil, and prayed over her. At first she took a turn for the worse, but dramatically improved after a few days and completely recovered!

My pastor handed me a huge volume on the teachings of Martin Luther, and encouraged me to take it home to read. He prayed with me before I left his office.

Later, at home, I curled up with the book and began leafing through the pages. I discovered that Luther endorsed healing prayer. *If it was good enough for Martin Luther, it's good enough for me.*

Healing Gigi wasn't going to be easy. After all, she'd been sick for many years. I didn't want to get her hopes up—only to be disappointed. I began praying, seeking guidance.

Gigi awoke with a familiar sore throat one Sunday morning. Ted and Shawn went on to church without us. When they returned, I was stroking Gigi's forehead as she shivered beneath a pile of blankets. *God please show us what to do.*

Nancy's words echoed: *"There might be something..."*

"Gigi... honey, would it be okay if a lady from church came to pray for you?"

Gigi nodded and whispered, "Okay."

"Let's take your temperature before I call."

I slid the glass thermometer between cracked, peeling lips. Conflicting thoughts taunted: *Don't call Phyllis, she's just a crazy fanatic! You don't want to get Gigi's hopes up, she'll only be disappointed. Isn't she suffering enough? What kind of mother are you anyway? Prayer won't do any good, so don't bother.*

"Mom, my throat hurts," Gigi mumbled. Fever glazed eyes reflected my miniature image. I removed the thermometer from her mouth. It was over *104 degrees*, but this was not unusual for her. She asked for another blanket. I tucked a quilt around her shoulders and brought her a drink. "Honey, drink some water."

After a small sip, she pushed the glass away. "It hurts too bad."

More thoughts battled for attention as I reached for the phone. After several rings Phyllis answered with a groggy, "Hello."

I explained that Gigi was sick again, and asked if she wanted to come and pray with her oil.

"W-e-l-l," she drawled, "I was just taking a nap. I'll pray and ask the Lord what to do."

"You mean, you might *not* come?"

"I'll see what the Lord instructs me to do," she said.

Honestly, does this woman have to pray about every move she makes— even about praying? "I hope you come, she's awfully sick. We missed church this morning."

"I'll let you know as soon as I have an answer."

We said our good-byes and hung up. A few minutes later I pushed the creaky screen door open and stepped outside for a bit of fresh air. The magnificent view of the fjord like bay and mountains calmed my spirit as usual. The blue sky was reflected in the placid water with barely a ripple. Sunlight and shadows playing on the lower mountain slopes triggered a familiar psalm: *I will lift up mine eyes unto the hills, from whence cometh my help* Psalm 121:1 (KJV).

"Please God, let her come—she just has to!"

When I heard the phone ringing I ran back into the

house. It was Phyllis. "I've decided to come and pray for Gigi. Is it okay if I bring my prayer partners?"

"Er..sure."

Phyllis continued: "Before we come I must ask you to do something."

"Okay, what?"

"Please remove anything from your home that might be offensive to the Lord."

"Offensive? Like what?"

"W-e-l-l"... she continued, "like statues of false idols, unclean books or magazines, Ouija boards. Ask the Lord to show you."

"I don't have any statues—but Gigi has an Ouija board. It's just a game isn't it?"

"Oh, no." Phyllis informed me, "Ouija boards belong to the occult. You must get rid of it."

"I have the book *The Exorcist*, should I get rid of that too?"

"Yes, take it out of the house. Have everything out by the time we get there so we can pray unhindered."

I promised I'd do my best, and then gave her directions to our home.

After our phone conversation, thoughts persisted: *You're not going to listen to that nut are you? There's nothing wrong with the stuff she objects to. It's not too late, call her back and tell her not to come! Do you want people to think you're crazy too?*

I was somewhat offended. *Who does she think she is anyway, accusing me of having evil in my house?* But, I reasoned, *perhaps I should humor her. Who knows? There could be something to this.*

21

I tossed a few books into a bag before rooting in Gigi's bedroom closet for the Ouija board. *This was expensive! You're not gonna get rid of a Christmas present are you?*

Ted observed my scavenger hunt, "What's going on?"

When I explained my actions he rolled his eyes heavenward and muttered, "Oh brother!" He went upstairs to his study. There was no turning back now. Even though Phyllis seemed a bit weird, I'd made my decision, and would follow through with it—come what may. I stashed my collection in the carport, hoping there was nothing else in the house that God didn't like because I'd removed everything I could think of.

When the doorbell rang I welcomed my guests. Phyllis smiled and offered her hand. Large round glasses magnified her shining eyes. Gray streaks laced through wavy brown hair. She introduced herself, her husband, and a woman who appeared to be in her early thirties, about my age. I ushered my guests into the house and offered them coffee which they politely refused.

Phyllis' husband walked to the bay windows to admire the view. Phyllis went to the sofa and knelt next to Gigi. They talked quietly for a few minutes before she said, "Jesus loves you very much, do you believe He can make you better?"

Gigi nodded, "Yes."

Phyllis' husband settled into a chair near the fireplace, closed his eyes, and began praying silently. Phyllis withdrew a small bottle of oil from her pocket and removed the cap. She poured a few drops into her hands and rubbed them together. With an oiled index finger she drew a shiny cross on Gigi's forehead. Next, she placed glistening hands on flushed cheeks and began to pray softly.

The other lady suggested I join her at the dining room table. I followed her lead and bowed my head while Phyllis continued praying. A few minutes later Phyllis rose to her feet. "We're finished now."

"That's all there is to it?" I asked.

"Yes, we've prayed, the rest is up to Jesus."

"Did you feel anything?" Her husband asked as he stood up.

"A strange thing happened." Phyllis said.

"What?"

"Well, I usually feel heat when I pray for healing, but Gigi is burning up with fever. When I prayed this time—my hands got cold. I believe God's power flowed into her."

"Isn't she suppose to leap up or something?" I asked. "What do we do now?"

"Just wait and see, there's a difference between a miracle and healing."

Phyllis explained, "A miracle is instantaneous, while healing may take some time. Does her fever usually spike at night?"

"Yes, nighttime is the worst."

"We'll take it as a sign that God touched her if the fever is down this evening. Call and let us know her temperature either way."

As the threesome walked towards the door I hated to see them go. A sweet, peaceful presence was leaving with them. As soon as they drove away Ted came downstairs. He seemed agitated. "Who were those people?"

"I told you — they're from church! They came to pray for Gigi."

"What for?"

"Because she's sick all the time! Why else?"

Ted stared at me as though I'd lost my mind. He shook his head, sighed and went outdoors. I didn't want to let on how disappointed I felt. Gigi looked no better than before they came. *Maybe I did make a mistake getting her hopes up.* My thoughts assured me that I'd been taken for a fool.

Gigi called me. "Mama, my throat hurts real bad, can I have an aspirin?"

"Sure." I said. Gigi grimaced as she swallowed the adult strength pill. "Drink more water," I urged, "you need the fluid."

"I can't," she whispered. She closed her eyes and sank back onto the pillow.

A few minutes later she was asleep. I busied myself with chores, checking on her every so often. Before long, strands of golden hair clung to beads of sweat on Gigi's forehead. *Good! The aspirin is working.* I gently removed the quilt—watching her chest rise and fall with each breath. She felt cool to the touch.

A while later she sat up, pushing the remaining covers to the floor. "Mama, I feel a lot better, Jesus made me well!" She picked up baby Ryan who played nearby. I chuckled at the contrast between the skinny girl and the roly-poly little boy squealing with delight. "It might just be the aspirin," I warned.

"Mama, can I have something to eat?"

"Are you serious?" *She's never had an appetite at this stage of the game.*

I served her soup, crackers, Jell-O, and 7-Up. She ate everything on the tray and announced: "I'm gonna take a shower and wash my hair now—I'm going to school tomorrow!"

Later, Gigi's rosy cheeks glowed as she stood before the mirror drying her silky hair. I wanted to believe Jesus touched her, but doubtful thoughts taunted. *Just wait till that aspirin wears off, she'll be so disappointed. That was stupid to call Phyllis and get Gigi's hopes up. You're really a terrible mother!*

Ted watched from a distance. I could just imagine the wheels turning in his engineer's mind.

Several hours later Gigi still felt cool. The aspirin had surely worn off by now! It was time for the test. I shook the thermometer vigorously before offering it to her. She stuck it beneath her tongue and we waited.

A few minutes later the thermometer's mercury line stopped at *98.6* degrees. *How peculiar.* Gigi's temperature was usually sub-normal following a bout of illness.

It was time to call Phyllis. She answered after the first ring. "How's our girl doing?"

"I just took her temperature. It's normal, 98.6!"

"Praise The Lord!" Phyllis exclaimed. "Wait just a minute!"

I could hear her talking to others as she gave them

the news. A chorus of **"Praise The Lord!"** echoed in the background. *She really is a fanatic,* I thought. I thanked her and promised to keep in touch.

When I tucked Gigi into bed that evening we offered a prayer of thanksgiving. I prayed fervently that she would be okay in the morning.

* * * *

Counterfeits

Gigi awoke early the next day. Though her throat still felt a bit sore she insisted on going to school. "Let's take your temperature again, just to make sure," I insisted. It was still normal. After school, Gigi bounded into the house and tossed her books aside. "My throat's all better now!"

Our encounter with answered prayer caused me to rethink my spiritual beliefs. Gigi and I both realized there was far more to faith than we'd imagined possible.

Phyllis was always there for me, answering questions, praying with me, and giving me books about the Holy Spirit. I learned that miracles were happening across the nation and around the world in the Christian community.

Several weeks later, Gigi awoke with a sore throat, fever, and chills. I was baffled—because by now, I was *sure* Jesus had healed her. A taunting thought scoffed: *You're a fool, God didn't heal her — you only thought He did!*

I called Phyllis to tell her the sickness had come back.

"W-e-l-l ... now..." she drawled in her casual manner. "God doesn't give healing and then take it back again. Let's ask Jesus to show us what's really going on here. It could be an attack from Satan to make you doubt the healing. It could be a counterfeit."

Phyllis prayed over the phone, asking the Lord to show us the answer. As I hung up the receiver, I remembered something. *The Ouija board!*

A few days after Phyllis prayed for Gigi's healing, I brought the board back into the house and put it away.

I asked God's forgiveness and promptly removed the board from the closet. I took it outside and headed for the garbage can. The Ouija board slipped from my hands and landed in some tall weeds. The NO corner emerged between blades of grass.

A phrase I'd often repeated in church came to mind. I spoke the words with fervor and authority: "*I renounce the devil and all his works and all his ways!*" With that I broke the board forcefully and tossed it into the garbage can.

That afternoon Shawn came home from school with a sore throat. Both children were vomiting and running fevers. I herded them into the station-wagon and gave them each a pail. I buckled Ryan in his car seat before we sped off towards the doctor's clinic.

The pediatrician discovered scarletina rashes on Gigi and Shawn's chests. He took throat cultures, and seemed so certain that it was strep he prescribed penicillin.

Both cultures came back positive for strep. The children responded to the antibiotics and recovered after a few days. The attack proved to be a very good counterfeit of Gigi's previous ailments. That was the last episode of sore throat and high fever for Gigi. The cycle of illness was now broken in her life forever.

But now, baby Ryan needed prayer. His ear infections began when he was only six-weeks-old. Ted and I had spent the night pacing the floor with our crying infant. The painful ear infections continued for a year and a half. He was scheduled to have tubes put into his ears. As the day for the procedure drew near, I asked Phyllis if she would pray and anoint Ryan with oil too. She was more than happy to do so.

Ryan slumbered in his car-seat as she prayed over him. A few days later I took him to the ear specialist for a pre-op visit. The doctor examined Ryan's ears and said they looked fine. He wouldn't be needing tubes after all. The troubling ear infections ceased.

Phyllis was such a blessing as she continued to nurture me. I asked her to pray with me to receive the fullness of the Holy Spirit. I wanted what she had. I also hoped she would pray for my deaf right ear. I'd lost hearing as a result of mastoid surgery six years earlier. I felt certain God would heal that too.

One sunny afternoon, Phyllis and I joined hands at my dining room table. She prayed that Jesus Christ would become the center of my life and home. (That wasn't how I thought she'd pray, but it was the first step necessary before I could continue on.)

She placed her hands over both of my ears and prayed for healing. I felt immense joy; as though we were standing in the presence of Almighty God.

After she left, I kept testing my right ear. I fully expected it to open at any moment. When I awoke the next morning a large chunk of wax clung to the right outer ear canal. I took it as a sign that God had heard our prayer, though I still couldn't hear out of that ear. Phyllis was surprised the ear hadn't opened, but we knew God had me in His hands as I began an awesome spiritual journey.

The whole family was becoming more interested in the Lord. As Ted noticed the difference in me he started asking questions. Though Ted had attended parochial school as a child, and been faithful in church attendance, this was new to him too. We began praying together.

I thought something special had happened to Pastor Nesse too, because now his sermons made a lot more sense. But it was because I was no longer in my spiritual stupor. My greatest desire was to draw closer to God in every way possible, but there was still something lacking.

* * * *

Sweet Surrender

It was a cold January morning. The older kids were at school and Ryan was napping. I could delay no longer—it was time to surrender! I knelt by my dining room window seeking God in a cobalt blue sky above snowcapped mountains. I asked His complete forgiveness as I yielded every area of my life, *even Saturday nights!* Next I prayed to be filled with His Holy Spirit.

It wasn't an earth shaking experience. I simply felt deep, enduring peace along with a calm assurance of God's love for me. With great joy I embraced the commandment to return His love with my heart, soul and mind.

As I basked in sweet serenity two strange words came to my lips. I repeated them over and over and wrote them down. I was curious to know if they meant anything. I searched dictionaries to no avail, I could not find any words like the ones I had spoken. A few weeks later I found my answer in a gigantic, two-volume dictionary set. The words meant *Almighty Master*. I was stunned. I'd never addressed God in such lofty terms.

As I stepped out in faith, voicing my new language, it began to flow fluently.

There was another difference in my speech. I was no longer comfortable using foul language or listening to dirty jokes. I read Ephesians 5:3-4 in the Living Bible; *Let there be no sex sin, impurity or greed among you..... Dirty stories, foul talk, and coarse jokes —these are not for you. Instead, remind each other of God's goodness and be thankful.*

Jesus was my first thought in the morning, and the last one before drifting off to sleep at night. A song was ever present as I praised Him. I began to sing new songs, songs from my heart. I cradled little Ryan rocking and singing until he fell asleep against my chest. He was such a dear little boy.

The mirror reflected a new radiance. Friends commented on the change in my expression. I was about to learn that being filled with the Holy Spirit included gifts as part of the package.

One frosty morning I sensed the Lord's voice for the first time: *Go out to your well house.* It was not an audible voice, but a distinct impression, a little louder than a thought. I seldom went to the well house in the winter and dismissed the idea, but the voice persisted, *"Go out to the well house quickly."*

I stopped what I was doing and got my coat. As I pushed the creaky well-house door ajar, I didn't see anything unusual. Just then, a stream of water spurted across the shed forming a puddle on the floor. I shut off the pump and ran into the house to call a repairman. *You said to thank you Lord, no matter what!*

A technician came right away and repaired the leak. Had I not discovered the leak our well would certainly have run dry and perhaps burned out the motor.

People have asked me "How do you know what you hear is the Lord's voice?" I can only direct them to scripture. Psalms 103 tells us that *We are His people, the sheep of His pasture.* In John 10:14-16 Jesus says, *I am the good shepherd; I know my sheep and my sheep know me— just as the Father knows me and I know the Father—and I lay down my life for the sheep. I have other sheep that are not of this sheep pen. I must bring them also. They too will **listen to my voice**, and there shall be one flock and one shepherd,* NIV. In the book of John, verse 10:27 Jesus says: *My sheep **listen to my voice**; I know*

31

them, and they follow me, NIV.

One morning while working in the kitchen, I sniffed an odor like hot oil. Our huge side-by-side refrigerator was warm inside. Ice cream oozed from cartons in the freezer and ice cubes floated in their trays. I unplugged the refrigerator, gave thanks to the Lord, and asked: *"What do I do now?"*

A picture of a circular fan flashed in my mind's eye. One of the blades was jammed with a crumpled wad of white paper.

That evening when Ted came home from work I asked: "Do refrigerators have fans?"

He answered, "A refrigerator has a fan to cool the motor." Together we unloaded food onto the counters. Instead of complaining about all the work, I praised God for our abundance. Ted and I carefully maneuvered the monstrosity to its side. Dust balls clung to exposed tubing. Then we saw it—a circular fan jammed by a crumpled wad of white paper.

"God showed you this?" Ted gasped.

He was fascinated with his new wife, never quite knowing what to expect when he came home anymore. He was most impressed by the joy that bubbled out of me.

The Lord began showing me creative ways to demonstrate love to my family. As I shared insights with Ted, he'd look towards the ceiling and mutter: *"Keep it coming Lord!"*

I listened to teachers on Christian radio, joined Bible studies, and read my Bible daily. I had so much to learn—I was like a dry plant soaking up water.

One afternoon friends asked me to join them for

a movie that had been filmed in Seattle. *Cinderella Liberty* was about a sailor who had fallen for a prostitute. The woman lived with her eleven-year-old son in a dingy apartment. The neglected boy often went hungry, eating only candy bars. Instead of milk he drank beer. The sailor bonded with the child.

I came home from the movie with a troubled heart. *Lord, is there some eleven-year-old boy you want me to minister to, besides my own?*

I was finishing my coffee one morning when the phone rang. A man's voice asked: "Is this Mrs. Genengels?" He identified himself as a social worker from California. "I'm calling about your eleven-year-old nephew, *Billy. He's currently a ward of the state of California and we're trying to find a foster home for him."

"Oh!"

"Your mother suggested I call you. It's usually better, if possible, to place a child with a relative, rather than a stranger."

I hadn't seen Billy since his parents divorced when he was three-years-old. I told the caller I'd discuss the proposal with my husband and get back to him. *Is this what you are trying to tell me Lord?*

Ted and I debated the pros and cons of Billy coming to live with our family. We learned that he'd been removed from his home more than once, and was considered a "handful." The social worker warned that it might take awhile for all the details to be worked out. Ted and I prayed with our children for God's will to be done.

Chapter Two

Prayer Partners

O ne morning an acquaintance from PTA, Ann
Krieger, called and asked if she could stop by.
I was delighted! Though happy spiritually, I was
lonely physically. Some of my former friends were
not exactly thrilled with my new outlook on life. I'd
been praying for a way to make friends with Ann.

We felt a kinship immediately. Ann's ready smile
and inner beauty matched her outer beauty. She
reminded me of Debbie Reynolds, the movie star. I
poured mugs of coffee and placed fresh baked cookies on the table. We talked about our children; she
had a girl and three boys. One of her sons was in
Gigi's class at school.

In her Texas drawl, Ann shared a recent experience. She'd attended a luncheon with a group known
as *Women's Aglow.* Her brown eyes sparkled as she
related how some ladies had prayed with her as she
rededicated her life to Jesus.

I shared about Gigi's healing and my recent experience with the Lord. We discovered that we'd both encountered God the exact same week in January!

I told Ann about my nephew, Billy, and asked her if she'd pray regarding the situation. That afternoon, a Roman Catholic and a Lutheran joined forces for their very first time as prayer partners.

A few weeks later, after a prayer session in Ann's kitchen, she asked if I'd mind stopping at the post office on my way home. As I picked up a stack of letters, Ann said "danke shoen."

"Hey, what does that mean? I say that a lot in my prayer language!"

Ann laughed, "I thought everybody knows what that means. It means 'Thank You' in German."

The languages, now flowing fluently, were not always the same. I seemed to pray in various dialects. Now when I sang the hymn *O For a Thousand Tongues* it took on a whole new meaning. My prayer language opened the door to more gifts of the Spirit.

I was given a copy of the book *Nine O'clock In The Morning*. It is a faith building story of how Father Dennis Bennett came to a small, struggling Episcopal church in the Norwegian community of Ballard, in Seattle. Through the power of the Holy Spirit, a thriving, world renowned church blossomed. The book encouraged me in my new walk with the Lord. I felt God's prompting to give a copy of the book to the president of our local PTA.

But, Lord—I hardly know the woman, what if she

thinks I'm crazy?

Each time I drove past Jane Berggren's driveway I felt convicted. I finally bought a copy of the book and took it to her home.

The attractive, green-eyed brunette greeted me at her door with a friendly smile. I explained why I was there as she curiously inspected the book's cover. She thanked me for stopping by.

A few days later Jane telephoned to say how much she'd enjoyed the book, especially since she was an Episcopalian. She asked if I'd like to go with her sometime to hear Dennis Bennett in person. Thus, our friendship was born.

Ann invited Jane and me to an Aglow luncheon held several miles away. We entered the banquet room to soft piano music. A smiling hostess ushered us to a table of women and introduced us. After a delicious lunch we stood to sing. I watched curiously as women clapped their hands to the beat of lively songs. They raised their arms heavenward as they sang slower songs. The leader explained, "Lifting our hands is a scriptural way of blessing the Lord as well as a sign of surrender."

I sensed sincerity, peace and joy coming from the women as they worshipped.

On the way home I remarked: "Though the speaker seemed a bit narrow minded, I enjoyed the meeting."

"Maybe we're supposed to become more narrow minded too," Jane said. I pondered her words. The following month we went again. Tears filled my eyes as we entered the room. The presence of the Lord was so obvious. Many of the women's faces radiated joy! When it came time for singing, I joined in. The songs were unfamiliar, but I quickly learned the choruses. One scripture song especially touched my heart. *"Thy loving kindness is better than life, thy loving kindness is better than life, my lips shall praise thee, thus will I bless thee, I will lift up my hands unto thy name."*

If my praise could bless the Lord (instead of always asking Him to bless me) I wanted to do so. I slowly raised my hands and looked around to see if anyone was watching me. Nobody was.

A strange thing happened when I entered an unfamiliar realm of worship. As I extended my hands towards God, I saw a very clear mental image of Jesus nailed to the cross. Tears coursed down my cheeks as I sang to my Savior. *So this is why they lift their hands!* Most of my adult life I'd been self conscious about my height of six feet. But as I worshipped I felt as small and insignificant as a grain of sand. I realized that I am exactly the height God created me to be.

Every time I raised my hands in worship, for months to come, I saw Jesus, either from a distance, or just his beautiful face.

I viewed the cross of Calvary from various perspectives. At times I stood looking up. Other times, I saw Jesus only partially from behind the cross. Sometimes I looked down from above — as perhaps the angels or our Heavenly Father might have watched Him. I observed the scene from the side too; but no matter how I visualized the crucifixion, it seared my heart.

After the meetings, I joined women lined up for prayer in response to the speakers' messages. I sought prayer for my deaf ear many times, but the Lord's answer was gentle: *"My grace is sufficient for you, for my power shows up best in weak vessels..."*

One morning the California social worker called regarding my nephew Billy. The paper work was completed; Billy would soon be coming to live with us.

* * * *

Invisible Scars

Ted and I left early one morning, with little Ryan, to meet Billy's flight at the airport. Traffic on I-5 was snarled and we were late. We frantically searched the nearly empty terminal before we spotted him exiting a rest room. The tow-headed child's innocent blue eyes and angelic smile disarmed me. I don't know what I expected, but he looked so vulnerable and lost. My last memory was of a chubby toddler stumbling over Christmas toys. "Billy?" I said.

"Aunt Carol? Uncle Ted?" he responded.

As we hugged I smelled a strong odor of cigarette smoke. *I'll deal with that later,* I reasoned. Billy had no luggage, only a few things in a paper bag. He took to little Ryan immediately, and hoisted him onto his shoulders.

We stopped at a restaurant on the way home. Billy wolfed down a cheeseburger, a large order of fries, and a giant chocolate milkshake. He chattered about his plane ride the rest of the way home.

Gigi and Shawn were home from school when we returned. They welcomed Billy with shy smiles and showed him to his room. I emptied his bag of tattered clothing, most of which didn't fit him anymore. The kids introduced Billy to our collie dog, Goggie. The shaggy dog wagged his tail and offered his paw before covering Billy's face with wet kisses. Later, Billy cuddled our half Siamese cat and renamed him "Teeger."

That evening I tucked the boys into their bunkbeds with a prayer and a kiss.

Billy wet the bed the first night. He was upset when I discovered the accident, but I assured him it was "No big deal."

My nephew proved to be a very disturbed child. Wetting the bed was a nightly ritual. He hoarded food under his bed and in closets. He helped himself to things that didn't belong to him. I confronted him one afternoon as he was taking money from my purse. "I want to send it to my Ma," he said.

One afternoon Billy came home carrying a large bucket labeled *Fish Hatchery*. He proudly showed off the chum salmon he had "caught." When asked how he caught it, he answered, "With a stick and a string off the bridge."

Lying was as natural to him as eating. Teaching the boy right from wrong seemed an insurmountable task. He was caught stealing candy, cigarettes, and snuff from the local store. Not only was he addicted to cigarettes, he chewed tobacco too.

Billy had a bad case of athlete's foot and couldn't

remember a day when his feet hadn't itched. A physical exam revealed that he was color blind. He'd never been to a dentist and his teeth needed fillings. Billy lapped up the special attention.

Billy's outgoing personality included a subtle charm. He sang the ditty: "McDonald's is your kind of place; they feed you rattlesnakes; they stuff 'em in your face ....they smear ketchup in your hair, so next time I go there ... I'll wear my underwear. Yum, yum, yum. I'm gonna get me some. McDonald's is your kind of place!"

He loved to get a laugh and attracted friends easily; other disturbed kids. I hoped his behavior would not rub off on Shawn.

Billy and Shawn signed up for Pee-Wee baseball. Our family attended their games, though the boys spent most of the time warming the bench. They joined Boy Scouts and began earning badges.

Billy's poor reading and writing skills left him significantly behind his fifth grade peers. After special education classes and tutoring he began making some progress.

Billy confided stories of abuse by various stepfathers. He told of being beaten, kicked, locked out of the house, denied food, and other horror stories. One incident took place when he was about six-years-old. He was ordered to clean a filthy garage littered with garbage, papers, bottles, cans, and junk of all kinds. Billy reasoned that hopping up and down might make the pile look smaller. While jumping, he sliced his foot on a can lid and ran crying to his stepfather.

"I'll fix that!" the man said. "How does this

feel?" he said as he poured a bottle of rubbing alcohol on the open wound. The burning pain seared Billy's trust as well as his foot.

The same man killed Billy's pet cat and hung it in the bedroom closet for him and his sister to discover. Billy's punishment for wetting his bed had been ice cold showers in the mornings. Billy alluded to sexual abuse, but would never discuss it openly. His life had been a mixture of perversion and pain. The cruel treatment left invisible scars on Billy's heart. My heart ached for him.

One afternoon as Shawn and a friend played in nearby woods they witnessed Billy performing an unnatural act with our dog. The boys ran home and reported what they'd seen. Their eyes widened as they related the details. I told them I'd deal with Billy when he came home.

I felt nauseous as I prayed *O God, how am I supposed to handle this one?* I went upstairs seeking Ted's advice. He was very uncomfortable with the subject and shrugged his shoulders, "I don't know."

We prayed a desperate prayer for wisdom. When Billy came home I asked him to come into Ted's study. Billy stared down at his shoes as I closed the door.

"The boys told me something they saw a little while ago."

"They're liars," he cried. "They're big, fat liars!"

I gently raised his chin and looked deep into anguished blue eyes.

"Are they lying Billy?" I asked— struggling to remain calm.

Tears rippled down his smudged cheeks. "No," he whimpered, wiping his nose on the back of his hand.

For a brief moment I felt like ringing his neck, but an overpowering emotion caught me off guard. I felt Christ's all consuming love for this child bubbling up from some deep reservoir within me. I drew Billy into my arms and held him close as we both cried. I'd never experienced such marvelous love for any human being before. As I embraced Billy, words tumbled from my lips. "God loves you more than you will ever know. He wants you to learn His ways."

I explained that sex was a gift given by God for marriage, but that sometimes people used the gift in the wrong way. I told him how each species is to mate with its own kind. Billy nodded in understanding.

Ted listened in stunned silence as I rambled on.

Billy and I went downstairs where the boys were playing a board game at the dining room table. We joined hands as I prayed for the Lord to remove the memory of the afternoon. Billy went to the beach alone to "talk to God." The boys did not bring up the incident again.

Over the next few days I pondered Billy's behavior. Ted and I weren't sure just what to do. *Should we get rid of the dog? Should we send Billy back to his mother? Was his behavior damaging to our children?* I felt certain the Bible must deal with this subject somewhere, but I didn't know where to look. I begged God to direct my path.

I tried opening the Bible randomly, but didn't get far. One afternoon, while on my knees praying, I saw a vision like a flashing neon sign: **Leviticus.**

Leviticus? Lord, is that in my Bible? I got my Bible and flipped through the pages until I found Leviticus. I could not find what I was looking for in the mysterious text. I got back on my knees and asked: *"Where in Leviticus, Lord?"*

As I awaited an answer, another sign flashed before me, a giant **18.**

I turned to Leviticus 18. Just about every sex sin imaginable is noted in that chapter. I suspected Billy had been exposed to many of them. I was amazed that God would show me so pointedly where to look. But why not? The Holy Spirit knows the Bible from cover-to-cover, *He wrote it.* I was awed by the apparent importance of the *Old Testament*, as well as the New Testament.

That afternoon I showed Billy the passage, and explained how God's Word provides guidance so we can learn how to follow Him. Billy seemed fascinated at the tailor made instruction from the Word of God. After that lesson I felt at peace, and I think Billy did too. We did follow up with professional counseling for Billy to address his problems.

Billy accompanied us to church, Bible school, evangelistic meetings and Christian concerts. He had many questions and seemed to have a receptive heart. He often responded to altar calls by going forward for prayer.

Ted and I took the children to Holden Village, a Lutheran retreat center in the heart of the Cascade mountains. We ferried up scenic Lake Chelan to a remote dock near the end of the lake. Ted planned to hike into the village with Gigi, Shawn, and Billy. I kissed the foursome good-bye as they set off with backpacks. Ryan and I rode a bus up switch-backs to the village surrounded by mountain peaks, forests, nature trails, streams and lakes. We joined visitors from across the United States for a quiet retreat with no cars, phones, or television. Little Ryan and I enjoyed the camaraderie of the village along with daily worship services.

A week later, the rest of our deeply suntanned family trekked into the village carrying freshly picked berries. The children rambled excitedly about their adventures with wildlife in nature's wonderland. We spent the next week all together at the village.

One evening everyone was summoned to the only cottage that had a TV. Young and old alike crowded around the snowy image of President Nixon giving his resignation speech that August evening in 1974.

As fall's golden days edged towards winter, I began praying about Christmas gifts for the children. Money was so tight. There never seemed to be quite enough to make ends meet. Billy was fascinated by Ryan's toys and was very hard on them. He was far too big for Ryan's riding toys as he awkwardly straddled them. Sometimes he bashed the toys to pieces. Before long most of them were broken.

Why Lord? Is this the thanks I get for taking this boy?

He reminded me of a scripture: *Give, and it shall be given unto you; good measure, pressed down, and shaken together, and running over, shall men give into your bosom. For with the same measure that ye*

mete withal it shall be measured to you again,
Luke 6:38 (KJV). *"As you give unto me I will
take care of Ryan."*

One morning a neighbor called on the phone. "I
was wondering— would you be interested in a few
toys that Kurt has outgrown?" Dolores asked.

I walked to her house—assuming she had three or
four nice toys to offer. Dolores opened the door and
greeted me with a smile. My jaw dropped at the sight
of her hallway. It looked like a toy store! Toys were
stacked everywhere: Fisher Price toys, numerous cars,
garages, trucks, riding toys, airplanes, games, books,
puzzles, etc., all in excellent condition.

I went home to get the station wagon and filled
the back with treasures. We had a huge sack of toys
left over to give to another family.

Christmas gifts abounded that year, but the best
gift of all was the realization of just how much Jesus
cares about every aspect of our lives.

Billy's mother began calling—begging him to
come back to her. Though Billy no longer wet the
bed, after her calls he had "accidents." He loved his
mother and struggled with his options as her calls
increased in frequency. Before long she regained
custody. Since she'd left the state of California, they
no longer had jurisdiction in the matter.

We said tearful good-byes at the airport and
promised to write. I must confess that a part of me
was relieved that Billy was going home.

A month or so later, Billy ran away from his
mother and got into trouble with the law. He lived
with his father for awhile before running off again.

When he was fourteen he came back to our home, against our better judgment. By this time he was incorrigible. He had no respect for rules, skipped school, came and went at all hours, and was verbally abusive. He fought with Shawn, and rough-housed with Ryan until he cried. Billy disappeared one morning, along with our camping gear and a neighbor's motorcycle.

They say "A good man dies when a boy goes wrong." Billy went on to live a life of crime and spent many years in and out of the penitentiary. Years later, he wrote saying that at some of the darkest hours in his life, in the hole at prison, he recalled things about God that gave him hope. I thank God for prison ministries. I know Jesus will complete the good work started in Billy. God has promised to never leave us or forsake us. I challenge anyone who reads this story to pray for him.

Chapter Three

A Triple Braided Cord

The Holy Spirit was our teacher as Ann, Jane, and I met to pray on a weekly basis. One of our first prayer requests was for a neighbor with a mysterious rash all over her body. As we joined hands and haltingly began praying out loud, God's presence filled the room. "It's just like being at an Aglow meeting!" Ann said.

We soon discovered the Lord's call on our lives, intercessory prayer. We met often to pray for our families, churches, pastors, neighbors, teachers, schools, bus drivers, and so on. We began by praising God, and asking the Holy Spirit's direction for our prayers. More than once, little Ryan fell asleep in my lap while we prayed.

Answers to prayer built our faith like nothing else. We saw changed lives, healed bodies, and people accepting Christ as Savior. We witnessed destructive habits and addictions broken, and loved ones set free. As we prayed for our families we ministered to each other.

The Lord taught us many things in those early days of intercession. He advised us to take advantage of our prayer time while we could, saying one day we would go in separate directions and be linked with others to pray. Jesus promised that all three of us would never be discouraged at the same time. One or two of us might be going through a trial, but never all three at once. He said we would be going to distant places as He had much to show us.

Our prayer sessions grew more intense and lasted longer. The more we prayed the harder it was to leave that realm of peace and revelation. These encounters encouraged our relationship with Him and each other.

At one of our prayer sessions, I saw (in the Spirit) an airplane whose panicked pilot was clearly in trouble. We prayed for the pilot and the people on board.

Later, that evening, I heard a news flash on my car radio. "Today a plane was forced to make an emergency landing — barely missing another fully loaded plane awaiting take off."

The next day there was a small article in the newspaper regarding the incident, titled "*Miracle.*"

Why God chooses to involve humans in the prayer process boggles my mind, but He does.

Jane was driving one drizzly morning as we approached Ann's house for a prayer session. She entered the driveway, shifted into park, and turned off the ignition. I had my hand on the door handle when Jane said, "Carol wait a minute. Before we go in, I want you to ask the Lord something."

I looked into distraught green eyes. "What is it Jane?"

"Ask Him if there's something I'm doing that grieves the Holy Spirit."

I was puzzled by her request. *She has to be kidding! Jane is the most disciplined person I know. She's up early each morning reading her Bible, and she's far more introspective and organized than I will ever be. What could it be Lord? Does she have some secret sin?*

"Okay, let's pray." I said. We joined hands in the stillness of the car. "Dear Lord, please show us if there is anything Jane is doing to grieve the Holy Spirit. We ask this in Jesus' precious name. Amen."

We sat quietly awaiting an answer, though truthfully I didn't expect one. Without warning, I sensed something like warm oil pouring over me. A euphoric current of God's immense love for Jane surged through me. I gulped back tears at the revelation I received. "Yes, Jane, there is something that grieves the Holy Spirit."

"I just knew it! Please tell me—what is it?"

"When you doubt His tremendous love for you — it grieves Him."

Little rivers spilled down Jane's cheeks as she nodded in understanding. I handed her a hanky as she whispered: "Oh Lord, please forgive me for ever doubting your love for me."

We entered our prayer meeting that day with a deeper appreciation for our Lord. It's so easy to believe God loves others, but to apply that love to ourselves is sometimes difficult. We feel unworthy.

After a prayer session in Jane's living room one morning, Jesus challenged the three of us: *"Confess your sins to one another that you might be healed."* One by one, we opened our hearts and shared some of our deepest secrets. Our vulnerability knit us together in a special bond as we prayed for healing and forgiveness. We trusted what we shared would remain confidential. Each of us experienced freedom from the bonds of the past. As prayer partners there could be no pretenses, no shallowness, nor any fear of being betrayed. God was preparing us for awesome things in the days ahead.

* * * *

Crown Him Lord of All

The Lord began talking to me about leading worship. My initial response was *no way, I could never do that!* I'd enjoyed singing as long as I could remember. As a child I hoarded numerous colorful plastic records. Later, when I discovered Mom's recording of *The Warsaw Concerto*, I listened endlessly. As a teenager I harmonized with the Everly Brothers, but I was no song leader. I'd barely made C's in high school chorus classes. I was too self conscious to lead children in singing—certainly not adults! I advised the Lord that He probably had me confused with someone else.

Women's Aglow was sponsoring a spring retreat. Jane and I decided to attend. Ann couldn't go but agreed to watch my older children.

The three of us met to pray a few days before the retreat. Ann had a promise for me... "God has a miracle for you this weekend, Carol."

I hoped my deaf ear might open.

The morning of the retreat, little Ryan had a tummy ache. When I dropped him at the home of his friend, he was still hurting. He wasn't feverish, but I wasn't sure if I should leave him or not.

My friend encouraged me; "Look Carol, God doesn't ask us to help friends only when conditions are perfect, just go and have a good time—he'll be fine."

I will ever be grateful to her.

Jane and I caught the Kingston ferry to Edmonds, on Puget Sound, and headed north up the freeway to Warm Beach Camp. Hundreds of women had gathered from across the state for the packed retreat.

The program began with dinner in a large dining hall. As we sang *The Doxology* in perfect harmony, a serene spirit of love settled over us. After dinner we gathered in a huge meeting room.

Aglow officers were seated on a platform in the front of the room. Regal banners representing different chapters decorated the walls around the auditorium. I held my new tape recorder in one hand, and my Bible in the other. The worship was wonderful and we listened to the best speakers we'd ever heard.

It was after midnight before Jane and I settled down. I tossed and turned most of the night. I missed my family and fears for their safety plagued me.

The next morning one of the workshop speakers had comforting words for our group. "The Lord has His eye on your families; they will be just fine." When she prayed for fear to leave in the name of Jesus, I felt immediate peace.

During evening worship I became painfully aware of my short comings. I repented of sins I was aware of, as well as those I was too blind to see. Saturday night I slept peacefully.

Sunday morning the auditorium buzzed with excitement as we filed in after breakfast. I placed my tape recorder on the floor and pushed the record buttons. A prolonged period of praise ushered us deeper into God's presence. A tremendous Spirit of worship prevailed as we sang: *"O for a thousand tongues to sing my great Redeemer's praise."* At the words, *"My gracious Master and my God, **assist me to proclaim...**"* my voice began to change. I struggled to restrain the unfamiliar surging power. *"He breaks the power of canceled sin, He sets the prisoner free ..."* My voice rose in a beautiful soprano. Our song leader led directly into the next hymn. *"All hail the power of Jesus' name, let angels prostrate fall. Bring forth the royal diadem and crown Him Lord of all."* I was no longer conscious of my surroundings—only a profound spiritual realm. Jesus was altogether glorious as angels lay face down before him. Another angel suddenly appeared bearing a tray with a resplendent crown. It was

Jesus' coronation day. Long lines, endless generations of all ages and races, streamed in from every corner of the globe to be present and accounted for.

My voice soared: "Go spread your trophies at his feet" ... I noticed awards of every kind: statuettes, crowns, jewels, mansions, medals, ribbons, advanced degrees; man's accomplishments, all meaningless in the presence of God Almighty.

It was a glimpse of heaven, and what is to come.

The recorder captured my ultra soprano voice blending with other voices throughout the auditorium. Something profound transpired as my perspective changed. I felt fully enveloped in Christ's love. *Truly, my cup runneth over.*

My ears weren't opened, but my eyes were!

At home I listened in awe at the beauty and power emanating from the tape recorder. *That's me?*

The Lord whispered: *"Now, will you lead singing for me?"*

"Yes Lord, I can do *all* things through Christ who strengthens me." God equips us to do what He calls us to do. A worship leader must first be a worshipper.

The days following the retreat I had little appetite. Later that week, at a banquet, I could only eat a few bites. "God, what's happening to me?"

He gently answered: *"I am causing you to be all that I created you to be."*

I shared the tape with anyone who would listen. Some wept; the power of God was so evident. The Lord encouraged me to share the tape with my mother and to give her a message from Him.

I played the tape in my parent's living room, and

delivered the message. "Mom, the Lord thanks you for giving me the gift of life." I told her how very much Jesus loves her. She dabbed her eyes with a tissue as Dad listened without comment.

A few days later I sat in Pastor Nesse's study playing the tape for him and Katie. "I *never* heard you sing like that before!" Katie exclaimed.

"The Lord told me I was *"Singing in the Spirit."*

"Yes," Pastor agreed, "That truly **is** singing in the Spirit!"

Pastor Nesse rejoiced at the wonderful things God was doing in my life. He was teaching a sermon series based on the book *Let Us Praise* by Judson Cornwall. He asked if I'd be willing to lead praise choruses, with my husband, on Sunday mornings. I promised we'd pray about it.

God speaks to us in funny ways sometimes. I was still a bit apprehensive about letting anyone hear my untrained voice. I had just started my car when a Carpenter's song came on the radio. *"Sing, sing a song, sing out loud, sing out strong. Don't worry if it's not good enough for anyone else to hear, just sing, sing a song!"*

Okay Lord, I guess it's time to step out in faith.

The scariest thing I ever did was face that huge congregation. Ted and I joined hands and began singing while Katie played the piano. As we stepped out in fear and trembling, hearts were touched. Some dabbed away tears as we led choruses.

Katie listened for the anointing to come on my voice, as on the tape, but it didn't happen. I realized that only in high praise could I sing like that.

We continued singing for several weeks until we were asked to stop. The associate pastor was uncomfortable with this type of music, and some in the congregation objected.

Pastor Nesse asked us to consider a Sunday evening service. It was decided to kick this off with a potluck. After making the necessary arrangements with the pastor we set the time. We hired a youth band from a neighboring church to play in the gym for the teenagers.

About forty adults gathered in the sanctuary after the potluck. I faced the crowd to give my testimony for the first time. As I began sharing about Gigi's healing, confidence replaced fear, and I felt strength flowing into me. I taught the reasons for lifting our hands, quoting scriptural reasons. After my talk I invited others to join me at the altar. When I finished praying and opened my eyes, I was astounded to see that every person, except one woman, had come forward. Men and women were kneeling at the altar and some wept as the Spirit of God touched their hearts. One lady, engulfed in deep grief since her husband's death, embraced peace and comfort that evening.

The next morning an elderly, retired public school teacher called me. "That's what it's all about isn't it?" she said. "The lifting of hands. I've read about it in Psalms for years, but last night it all made sense."

"Thank you, I am glad you were blessed."

As news of the event spread, I was approached by a member of the evangelism committee. "You should have gone through our committee, you know! You can't just take things in your own hands like that!"

But the pastor had given me permission, I didn't know anything about any committee. When I related the admonition to Pastor Nesse, he bellowed. "If we'd gone through that committee it wouldn't have happened at all!"

Our Sunday evening prayer and praise sessions continued for quite awhile. Several members of the congregation shared their testimonies. Sometimes Ted came with me, but usually he was home studying towards his master's degree.

Pastor Nesse was always there with us. How I praise God for him. Not everyone favored the movement sweeping the mainline churches. Congregations were splitting in many denominations as charismatic renewal spread throughout America. Many were told the movement was evil, and some charismatics were asked to leave their churches. A well-meaning woman warned me that my experience might be of the devil. I knew her concern was genuine, she just did not understand.

One Sunday morning Pastor Nesse addressed the congregation. "As many of you know, there are several in this congregation who have the gift of tongues. I don't operate in this gift, and the majority of you don't have this gift. My advice to you is this: 'Those of you who don't speak in tongues— refrain from judging those who do. Furthermore, those of you who do speak in tongues, don't judge those who do not! As you sit, side-by-side in church, respect each other's right to worship as he or she sees fit. ***There will be no division in this church!*** " he declared. And there was none as we heeded his wise advice.

I soon realized that it doesn't matter what spiritual gifts people claim to have if they don't operate in love. Jesus said His followers would be known by their fruits. Fruits such as love, joy, peace, patience, gentleness, goodness, kindness, faithfulness, and self-control are the true marks of a Christian. Without love the gifts often become a source of pride and arrogance. Our gifts must be used to bring Glory to God, not draw attention to ourselves.

Ted and I attended conferences on the Holy Spirit held in neighboring cities. Powerful testimonies inspired us and we worshipped for hours. Much inner healing took place as we learned the importance of walking in forgiveness and love.

Our church hosted a series of renewal weekends where Lutherans from neighboring towns came together as a team to share their faith. Ted and I were asked to join the Lutheran Lay Renewal team. We met wonderful people as we ministered in various churches. Our children benefited from the programs for the youth. At one event Gigi dedicated her life to Christ and said she wanted to spend the rest of her life serving Him. She began helping in Sunday School classes for handicapped children. Gigi has a gift for communicating with children and the kids loved her.

Shawn also gave his life to the Lord after a Billy Graham movie. Both children were active in the church youth group. Ryan usually tagged along with me wherever I went. He was a happy, compliant child who could entertain himself for hours with a few miniature cars. My life seemed full and more peaceful than I'd ever known. It was the lull before the storm.

Chapter Four

Compromises

Gigi was enjoying her fourteenth summer with her best friend Lisa. The two were inseparable as they romped on our beach, or rode horses at Lisa's ranch. They spent their days swimming, herding cattle, riding mini bikes, and practicing cheers for next year's try-outs.

Ted and I planned a family camping vacation at a Christian retreat center in Oregon. Gigi didn't want to go and asked to stay with her friend. Lisa could have come along, but Ted's dad was going with us, and there was no more room in our car. We convinced Gigi that she would enjoy herself making friends with teens at the center.

We packed our camping gear into the station wagon and headed south. Several hours later we reached our destination.

The retreat center is nestled in a forest abounding with waterfalls and nature trails. We were welcomed to the lodge by the camp's friendly hosts. We watched in fascination as they pointed out white doves circling the sun decks. Though we were camping, our meals would taken in the dining room with the other guests.

Gigi and Shawn raced ahead as we set out to explore the woods. Ted's dad followed them. Ryan sat perched on Ted's shoulders. His dimpled arms clung tightly as they approached a waterfall's cooling mist. "Daddy, Daddy, we're gonna get wet!" After they passed behind the falls Ryan cried out: "Praise the Lord! We didn't get wet!"

I lagged behind savoring the woodsy scent of bark and evergreens. Twigs and pine needles cracked beneath my feet. An occasional squirrel scampered across my path. There was a sense of serenity as sunlight filtered through lofty, overhead branches.

Inspirational speakers, prayer, singing and fellowship made the camp truly a place of renewal. Families sat around tables in the packed dining room. Teens sprawled on the floor and leaned against the walls as I gave my testimony one evening. The room was quiet as I shared from my heart. I told about Gigi's healing and our adventures with Billy.

The next day the camp directors took us aside. "There's something we'd like the two of you to pray about." Ted and I sat quietly as the man explained. "There's a fourteen-year-old girl here who desperately needs a foster home. *Tonya's been in trouble with the law, had some problems with drugs and alcohol, but she's really trying to turn her life around. Her mother, a lesbian, lives with another woman. Tonya doesn't want to live with them. Would you consider taking her? You might be an answer to prayer."

Ted and I made eye contact. "We could pray about it." I said.

A little while later Gigi ran up to us. "Mom, Dad, meet my new friend Tonya. Oh Mom, she needs a foster home, can we take her, please? Please? We're already good friends, it would be just like having a sister!"

"Honey, I don't know. We have to pray about this."

Tonya, a tall curvaceous blonde, flashed a vibrant smile revealing the straightest, whitest teeth I'd ever seen. Long, thick lashes framed her electric blue eyes. She was a knockout.

"I'd be the perfect daughter!" Tonya cooed before the girls ran off together.

Ted and I strolled hand-in-hand down a woodsy trail, until we came to a clearing with a bench. We sat down and began praying for guidance. The silence was shattered only by the squawk of a crow. After a few minutes, I heard the Lord's voice: *Do not suffer this child to come to you at this time. This is not in my plan for your family.*

I shared my impressions with Ted. He nodded in agreement.

I pictured Gigi's pleading eyes, the hopeful directors, and Tonya's perfect smile. I opened my Bible randomly to Matthew. 19:14. *"Suffer little children, and forbid them not, to come unto me: for of such is the kingdom of heaven"* (KJV).

But, I 'd clearly heard Jesus say: ***Do not suffer** this child to come.*"

That evening the hosts asked if we had an answer yet. I wanted to please them, and the girls who continued to beg us. "Maybe we can work something out," I ventured.

I thought of our neighbors *Betsy and *Dan Parker. The couple had often talked of taking in a teenage girl to help out with their three children. It seemed like a good compromise to me. I would soon learn a very painful lesson about compromising obedience to God.

Gigi sulked most of the drive home because Tonya couldn't live with us.

The next day I contacted the Parker's regarding the possibility of Tonya becoming their foster child. Betsy and Dan seemed interested, but wanted to think it over. They called later wanting to know more information. I advised them to contact the directors of the retreat center.

Less than a month later, Tonya came to live with the Parker family.

The Parker's three children danced up and down when Tonya arrived. They led her to a cozy bedroom in the basement of the waterfront home. It was every girl's dream room. Betsy had taken great care to prepare an inviting room with matching bedspread, pillow shams, and curtains for the windows. The children eagerly showed Tonya around the rest of the house. The next week was spent getting to know the family. Tonya's stories of her troubled life shocked the Parker's and they were determined to help the girl.

Gigi and Tonya soon became as thick as thieves, going everywhere together. Their jaunts seldom included Gigi's friend, Lisa, who found solace in her boyfriend.

Before long Tonya grew bored with the Parker's family routine and began running with a wild, older crowd. She thought nothing of hitchhiking and getting into cars with strange men. She introduced Gigi to all of her friends; older guys, alcohol, marijuana, and drugs. Our loving daughter turned sullen and rebellious before our very eyes. She began sneaking out at night and skipping school. More than once she came home with bloodshot eyes, reeking of sickly sweet pot. Tonya introduced Gigi to a guy old enough to be her father.

Ted and I spent sleepless nights after discovering Gigi's bedroom to be empty. We prayed daily for her safety and protection.

Realization jolted me like a cold shower. *My God, what have I done? I brought this on by disregarding your instructions. Do not suffer this child to come... that's what you said Lord! This was not your plan for our family.* How I longed to know *His* plan.

The Parker's tried restricting Tonya, but lying and sneaking around was an ingrained lifestyle. When Ted and I grounded Gigi, she lashed out, saying she hated us.

Late one night I checked Gigi's room only to find it empty again. Ted and I spent the next few hours praying until I could no longer keep my eyes open. I placed Ryan's large Tonka truck in front of the entry door so we could hear when Gigi came home. I wearily gave my burden to God, climbed into bed, and lapsed into a fitful sleep.

Ted sat up all night contemplating his life and praying. The sun was up when the door crashed into the toy truck. Gigi tossed her coat aside, ran to her room and locked the door. Ted woke me and we went to her room together. Gigi refused to answer us or come out. Later I checked her coat pockets and found a small plastic bag of something that looked like dried grass.

I quizzed Gigi until I learned the truth. She was madly in love with her boyfriend and wanted to marry him. I got nowhere trying to reason with her. Neither Ted, nor I knew how to handle our child. Ted was especially lost due to years of burying himself in work and studies. He tended to ignore problems until he exploded in anger. His actions built a great wall between him and the kids.

My prayer partners, Ann and Jane, continued to pray with me for Gigi. A cloud of worry and despair threatened my sanity. *Could this possibly be the same child Jesus healed of a chronic illness? Was she healed only to live a lifestyle like this?*

My efforts to deal with the Parker's seemed fruitless. They were ill-equipped to handle Tonya, and in their frustration blamed me, understandably so. I learned that disobedience to God rarely affects just one person, the consequences go far and wide.

Gigi's girlfriend, Lisa, asked her to be her maid of honor. She was marrying her boyfriend at the age of fifteen. Gigi wanted to get married too.

A group of women met at my home to pray. The

words we sang became my heart's cry that day. *"Unto Thee, O Lord, do I lift up my soul...O my God, I trust in thee: Let me not be ashamed, let not mine enemies triumph over me"* Ps.25:1-2 (KJV).

I dropped to my knees, asking forgiveness for compromising God's direction. *The righteous cry, and the Lord heareth, and delivereth them out of all their troubles. The Lord is nigh unto them that are of a broken heart; and saveth such as be of a contrite spirit* Ps. 34:18 (KJV).

A calm assurance that things would somehow work out settled over my heart.

A few days later, while praying, the Lord told me to forgive Gigi's boyfriend.

But why Lord? I hate him, he's ruined her!

It's vitally important that you obey— release him to me.

Though I still didn't understand, I knew better than to argue. I didn't feel like forgiving the man, but I made a conscious decision of my will to do so.

The next day we heard the news. Gigi's boyfriend had been killed the night before in a fiery automobile crash. His sports car was wrapped around a telephone pole.

Gigi was inconsolable. I took her to our church later that afternoon. She ran into the empty sanctuary and knelt at the communion rail. Guttural cries of anguish reverberated throughout the building as she poured out her grief.

Gigi begged to attend his funeral. Ann and I agreed to accompany her to the chapel. She sat between us as she joined a number of other teenage girls sobbing throughout the service.

Gigi sank into depression in the weeks to come. She was so despondent she wanted to die too. "We were going to be married someday!"

Nothing I said could mend her broken heart. I invited her to an Aglow meeting with me one morning. She agreed to accompany me since she could miss school. She sat stoically as a young minister testified about his teenage rebellion and God's forgiveness.

One sunny Saturday morning, Ted's birthday, Gigi left a note. She was running away. I called Ann and she came over. We sat in her car praying for guidance. After phoning some of Gigi's acquaintances, we learned of a party being held somewhere in the woods. Ann and I drove unfamiliar dirt roads until we found the clearing. Dozens of teens dressed in bell bottoms and psychedelic shirts were gyrating to wild music. A young man with long, flowing hair and a beard walked towards our car. He sipped foam from a paper cup full of beer. I asked if he knew where Gigi was. He offered to find her.

Gigi flushed with embarrassment when I urged her to get in the car. Tonya told us to "Get lost!" while a crowd observed the confrontation.

"I'm never coming home!" Gigi yelled before she turned and ran off into the woods. Ann and I finally drove away in defeat.

Gigi didn't return home that night or the next. I had no idea where she was. Days turned into weeks. Ted and I felt an overwhelming sense of failure and grief at our lack of parenting skills. We continued to pray.

I learned that Gigi was staying with a gang of rebels in a tiny, run down beach cabin near the local grocery store. *God—whatever it takes, please bring her back to You— and to us.*

Ted and I got conflicting advice. "Leave her alone, she will eventually return like the prodigal son in the Bible."

"Tough love! — have her arrested."

"Go get her, force her to come home."

"Throw her out again if she does come back."

I wrote Gigi a letter detailing my love for her, begging her to return home. I kept clinging to my only hope, Jesus.

One morning, while praying with my prayer partners, Ann said: "The Lord has a promise for you, Carol: 'One day Gigi will return to Him, and she will rise up and call you blessed.'"

I tucked the comforting words into a distant corner of my heart.

One afternoon I trudged up the driveway to the mailbox, in hopes that Gigi might have answered my letter. I spotted a wilted, dirty name-tag lying on the ground. It was from the Aglow meeting we had attended. I picked it up and read the scripture promise beneath Gigi's name: *If we confess our sins, he is faithful and just to forgive us our sins, and to cleanse us from all unrighteousness* 1 John 1:9 (KJV).

I closed my eyes and uttered yet another prayer. A vivid picture of a crimson drop of blood flashed in my mind. I heard Jesus say: *"That's the drop I shed for her. That's all it takes. Release her to me. She's mine you know. You gave her back to me the day she was baptized. The blood availed for her will never lose its power.*"

Bottled up tears found release as His words ministered to my broken spirit. I had naively thought I'd be the perfect mother—not repeating the mistakes my mother made with me. I recalled the first time Gigi was placed in my arms, and a part of my heart was captured forever. "I thought my tremendous love for her would be enough Lord," I whispered.

I heard Him gently say, "*Join the club.*"

Later that day, Shawn came home jabbering a mile a minute. He'd been fishing near the cabin where Gigi lived. He confessed that she'd given him an alcoholic drink, and a joint to smoke. "She said to come back later for a pill that will make me feel *really* happy!"

Things had digressed too far. Our prodigal showed no sign of returning, and now her behavior was affecting her brother.

Ted drove to the cabin, determined to bring our wayward child home. He knocked on the door of the run down hovel. A man opened the door and said Gigi was not there. Ted asked him to tell her he was looking for her.

When Ted came home we faced one of our most painful decision ever as parents. I recalled a teaching I'd heard. (*Sometimes we have to love our children enough to let them hate us for awhile.*)

We telephoned the sheriff and asked to have our daughter arrested.

An officer agreed to send someone to talk to us.

An hour went by and nothing happened. Ted called again.

"We'll get to it as soon as we can, it's been a busy night."

Another hour passed before anyone showed up. I believe this delay was in God's perfect timing. (We later learned that Gigi had been at the top of our driveway, letter in hand, deliberating about whether to come home or not. She decided to return to the cabin.) Finally, a deputy arrived at our home and took a report.

It was after eleven when the officer arrested a very stoned, angry girl and took her to juvenile detention. Ted and I slept fitfully in between prayers of relinquishment.

The next morning I tucked Gigi's Bible in my purse and went to see her. My heart pounded as I parked in front of the newly built juvenile facility. A uniformed guard informed me that Gigi couldn't have visitors, and nothing was allowed in her room. The tiny cell contained only a bunk and a blanket. She had to earn sheets, a pillow, a chair and anything else she needed.

"Can I please leave her Bible?" I asked.

The woman shrugged. "I guess a Bible's okay. Come with me."

I followed the guard down the corridor past closed doors. She removed a ring of keys from her belt and unlocked the door to Gigi's room.

I barely recognized the hollow-eyed child sitting on the stark plastic mattress. I wanted to hold her in my arms and tell her how much I loved her. There was such a chasm between us. At least she was safe, I knew where she was.

The guard handed the Bible to Gigi. "Your mother wants you to have this."

Gigi shot me a look of hatred before she tossed the Bible on her bed.

How have I failed so badly as a parent? I cried as I drove away from the institution that now housed my first born child.

Over the next few days Gigi had plenty of time for reflection. She later told me that out of sheer boredom she picked up the Bible and began to read. God directed her to Romans 13, regarding submitting to governing authorities as well as to God. He ministered comfort to a broken hearted girl through the pages of that holy book.

Finally, the day came for us to bring our daughter home. Ted parked our car behind the detention center before we made our way to a small, bleak office. We waited on a wooden bench facing a bare window. Relentless raindrops pelted the glass pane with a steady beat. A rhythm that seemed to hammer out failure, failure, failure.

Could this really be happening to our family? I felt like my world was crumbling around me. Nothing had prepared me for this moment. Ted's shoulders slumped in worry and defeat.

The director of the facility and a social worker entered the room. We were admonished to seek family counseling. The social worker handed us a business card with a therapist's name on it. "Hopefully you can work things out," she said.

Gigi was brought into the room. Her sullen expression shut us out as she avoided looking at us. The three of us left the building through a side door facing the parking lot.

We forged our way through the drizzling rain, each encapsulated in our own painful world. Ted and I felt certain we'd alienated our daughter for life. When we reached the car, Gigi's facade crumbled as she burst into tears. "I'm so sorry," she cried, "so, so sorry."

We opened our arms in unison as the three of us huddled together under soggy skies. Raindrops mingled with the tears on our cheeks.

Chapter Five

The Battle Rages

*F*amily therapy forced us to confront many of our parenting mistakes. It was painful and humbling to face the insights counseling revealed. Looking inward was like dealing with a festering boil; a sore needing cleansing before healing could begin.

I often shrieked at the kids the way my mother had done with me. Ted's pattern of working, studying, and teaching college classes left little time for the family. He was exhausted and irritable much of the time. I would vent my frustrations on him when he came home, and he overreacted—lashing out at the kids.

We learned better communication techniques with each other and our children. We set aside time to listen to one another, without interrupting, and to voice back what was said. Ted invited Gigi on dates for coffee and dessert so they could talk. He made more time for Shawn too.

We were encouraged to be more demonstrative with our children. Ted and I grew up in homes where affection was seldom displayed. We both lavished love on our kids when they were little, but as they grew older we somehow backed off. We were challenged to not let a day go by without telling our children we loved them. It seemed forced and unnatural at first, but as we allowed God's love to flow through us, it became easier.

As Gigi and I grew closer, she began to confide in me. One afternoon she felt free enough to tell me how she thought she'd disgraced the family so much that we wouldn't want her back. I assured her that nothing could ever stop us from loving her. "What others think just doesn't matter." I told her.

Tonya continued to be a problem. She was running wild, skipping school and hiding alcohol in the locker she shared with Gigi. Gigi admitted that she found it difficult to escape the hold that Tonya had on her.

I battled migraine headaches, gynecological problems and sleepless nights. At times I felt as though I could barely put one foot before the other. I challenged God one afternoon: *Lord, I'm so weary. Please, speak to me through a dream. I must hear from you today—I'm at the end of my rope.*

I slumped on my bed, closed my eyes, and drifted off. The Lord gave me the dream I asked for.

Ted and I were standing in the Parker's living room with Betsy and Dan. Tonya's birth mother and a social worker were also there. I looked around the room. "God is not in this house." I said.

Dan Parker looked me directly in the eyes. "God is too in this house!" he said, "let's pray."

We all knelt in a circle to pray. Jesus appeared in our midst and spoke: "The Lord giveth and the Lord taketh away. The Lord will send this one away."

I awoke knowing that God was going to intervene.

Gigi came home from school a few days later in a state of agitation. Tonya had been caught drinking at school and was suspended.

I had to do something! I decided to call Tonya's social worker and tell her what was happening. I began dialing the number but was distracted: *"Carol, put the phone down. Let Me handle this!"*

I sighed and hung up the receiver. *"Okay Lord."*

A few days later Gigi and I were conversing over a cup of tea when the doorbell rang. Gigi went to answer it. "I'll only be a minute Mom, it's Tonya."

I peered through the window as the girls argued beneath the apple trees. Tonya was wearing a tee-shirt, Osh Kosh overalls and a back-pack. Gigi glanced towards the house and back at Tonya. The next thing I knew—they were both gone.

I called Betsy to see if the girls had gone there. She said Tonya was supposed to be in her room. I waited while she checked and discovered that Tonya was gone. We agreed to call if either of us heard from them.

Mom and Dad's car pulled into our driveway. They were coming for dinner. I greeted them with the news, "Gigi's run off again, I just know it!"

Dad shook his head and sighed, "Not again!"

Ryan ran up to his Grandpa and grabbed his hand. As we entered the house I shot a silent, desperate prayer heavenward. Mom suggested I phone the ferry terminal to see if the girls went there. I heard the Lord's voice distinctly: *"Not yet."*

"Later, Mom, I'll call later."

Ted came home from work and greeted my parents. He kissed me as Ryan ran between us and wrapped his arms around his daddy's legs. Ted's smile quickly faded when I voiced my suspicions.

Mom mashed potatoes while I put the rest of the dinner on the table. We picked at our food and waited. Mom persisted, "Why don't you call the ferry terminal?"

Again, I heard the Lord's voice. *"Not just yet!"*

After dinner we watched the news on television. *"Now Carol!"* Jesus said, *"Call the ferry terminal now."*

Mom was relieved that I was finally taking her advice as I dialed the number. A man answered. "Bremerton Ferry Terminal."

"I...I was wondering if you might have seen two teenage girls." I described what they looked like and how they were dressed. "I just sold 'em tickets a minute ago," he said. "In fact, they were a nickel short so I made up the difference."

"They're run-aways!" I said.

`"Don't worry, they won't get on the boat."

"What should I do now?"

"Look—I'll call the police. The station's right around the corner. They'll take the girls there and you can pick 'em up."

I thanked the man before hanging up. I then called the Parker's to tell them where they could find Tonya.

Mom and Dad stayed with the boys while Ted and I headed for the police station. We parked the car, went inside and gave the man on duty our names.

An officer brought Gigi out. Her eyes were red and swollen from crying. "Mom, I'm so scared!" She said as she ran into my arms. I kept my arm around her as we walked to the car: "I kept praying—for God to help me," she said between sobs. "I didn't want to go to Seattle, but I couldn't seem to say 'No.'"

"God heard your prayers, honey." I said.

On the ride home Gigi told us how they hitchhiked to the ferry terminal, and pooled their change. "I hope I never see her again," she said.

A few days later Tonya's social worker removed her from the Parker home. She was finally out of Gigi's life for good.

* * * *

A Time To Heal

Gigi returned to church and resumed her duties helping with handicapped children's Sunday School. Pastor Nesse tutored her privately so she could be confirmed with her classmates. On confirmation day we celebrated with family and friends. A special cake and balloons helped to make it a festive event.

As the school year drew to an end, Gigi prayed about a summer job. She learned of an opening at Baskin-Robbins ice cream store.

"That sounds like fun!" I said.

"Yeah, I could eat all the ice cream I wanted. But I don't think that's the job God has for me."

Charleen, a friend from church, suggested Gigi apply at a summer camp near Tacoma. Gigi filled out an application and waited. Before long she was offered a job as a camp hand at Lutheran Outdoor Ministries. The job included room, board, and a very small stipend. She was to assist camp staff, and help with manual labor jobs.

Gigi fidgeted nervously on the drive to Tacoma. We received friendly greetings from staff, and Gigi was shown to her quarters. We kissed her good-bye and prayed over her. I knew she was still vulnerable, needing lots of tender loving care. So much of her sparkle had disappeared along with her innocence. We promised to keep in touch by letters and phone calls. I had peace about leaving her at camp, but I shed a few tears anyway as we drove away.

The camp minister, Pastor Wayne, proved to be a warm and caring shepherd of his flock. Pearl, the cook, took Gigi under her loving wing. The staff was comprised of dedicated young adults who loved the Lord.

Gigi worked hard sanding and painting fences. The experience of campfire singing, daily devotions, and Christian fellowship helped mend her heart. At the end of summer Gigi returned home closer to her Lord.

Her Junior year was a difficult one. Though she no longer ran with the wild crowd, she was branded as "one of them." She did have one good friend at school. Gigi studied hard and pulled up her grades. She attended church youth group and corresponded with friends from summer camp.

The following summer she returned to camp, this time helping in the kitchen. The work was grueling, but she learned a lot. Some staff members visited our home between sessions to fellowship, do laundry, and dig clams on the beach.

Gigi's Senior year was the loneliest time of her life, especially when her friend moved away. Lunch hours were sometimes spent huddled in a rest room stall rather than eating alone in the cafeteria. She often walked to her grandparents' house for lunch. Repentance required a high price because she no longer fit in with the crowd. She used the opportunity to improve her grades as graduation grew near. Gigi was a beautiful young woman. She was tall and slender with shoulder length honey blonde hair and large hazel eyes framed by long curly lashes.

Her high school graduation was a joyous occasion. Friends and relatives attended the celebration. A few days later she landed a job as a cook at a local restaurant.

A waitress invited Gigi to share an apartment and she moved in with her. She was independent and loving it. As her life began to turn around, Shawn's problems surfaced. Our trials with him would further test our faith.

Chapter Six

Praise

Shawn, a shy, serious kid was two years younger than Gigi. People often did a double take at the darling little boy with jet black hair, creamy skin, and large blue eyes.

As a toddler he was determined to master skills all by himself. When I tried to help him dress, or tie his shoes he would protest, **"I do it myself!"**

Three-year-old Shawn tripped while running towards me with outstretched arms. The blow to his forehead sounded like a watermelon hitting cement. I cradled him for hours while he cried and vomited. The goose egg resulted in a concussion that left him with severe migraine headaches.

When Shawn learned to draw and paint he went door-to-door selling his art work for a nickel or a dime. When he was older he sold garden seeds earning prizes.

School didn't come easy for Shawn. He struggled

with dyslexia, a short attention span, and impatient teachers. In the fifth grade he attended classes at a local eye clinic to help his eye-hand coordination. He spent afternoons jumping on a trampoline while batting at baseballs suspended from the ceiling. He worked numerous puzzles to stimulate his mental processing. The end result was that he became a pretty good reader.

Shawn entered a district wide art contest: *The Joy of Seeing*, where he won second place with a painting of an orange sunset seascape. Shawn's greatest joy was fishing in a row boat with his grandpa Andy.

At thirteen Shawn began spending a lot of time in his room. He seemed depressed as he struggled in school. Changing classes in junior high only added to his frustration. He lost things and forgot to attend his music lessons. He was often in trouble with his teacher and got the brunt of his paddle more than once. My efforts to have him transferred to another home-room teacher were unsuccessful.

Shawn lost interest in Boy Scouts and no longer looked forward to the outings. In baseball he often confused the coaches' signals because of the dyslexia. He wanted to quit the team, but Ted felt that he should finish what he'd started. After a heated argument Shawn ran off. When he didn't return that evening we were frantic. Ted and I searched everywhere and called the police. We spent the night praying and walking the floor. I imagined all the awful things that mothers think when their kids are missing.

The scout troop was also searching for Shawn.

On the third morning a neighbor stopped by to see if we had heard anything yet. When I said "No" she asked: "Well, what are you going to do, Carol?"

"I don't know what else to do, except pray. He's in God's hands."

"Honestly!" she said. Her expression told me what she thought of my logic.

That afternoon tears blurred my vision as I drove home from the police station. I was listening to praise music on the car radio when I heard the Lord's gentle voice: *"Praise me, even in these circumstances, Carol."*

As I began singing along with the radio a curious sensation of joy penetrated my pain. When I arrived home the phone was ringing. It was the neighbor who had been at my door earlier that day. She was calling from a department store in downtown Seattle. "I've just found Shawn!" she said.

"You have? Where?"

"You're not going to believe this, but I found him shopping in the Bon Marche!"

"The Bon Marche! Is he okay?"

"He's seems to be just fine. I was on my way to the University District when I decided to stop downtown. I don't know why I came here really, I wasn't planning to. Well, anyway the next thing I knew—there he was. Can you believe it?"

I thanked her and God simultaneously.

"I have to run now," she said, "I'll let you talk to the security guard."

I told the officer that Ted and I would catch the next ferry to Seattle. He said if we couldn't make it by six to go to the juvenile detention center downtown.

By the time we found the juvenile facility Shawn was locked behind a metal door with a small window. His blue shirt was drenched with blood from a nosebleed. Shawn began to cry as Ted and I wrapped our arms around him. "Shawn we were so worried."

"Mom, Dad, we've got to find Wilma! She doesn't know where I am. She'll be worried."

"Wilma? Is that where you've been, with Wilma?"

"Yes—but Mom, they wouldn't listen when I said she was waiting for me."

He frowned. "They made me come here! To jail! I didn't do anything wrong, they searched my pockets and everything!"

Wilma. The elderly spinster had idolized Shawn ever since he was a little boy, and he often visited her. It never crossed my mind that he might have gone to her, but it made sense.

"Let's get out of here!" Ted said.

We drove back to the department store where Wilma was frantically pacing back and forth on the street corner.

The four of us went to a restaurant to discuss the situation over dinner. Shawn had told Wilma that we went to New York and left him behind. She believed him! While we worried at home, they'd had a grand time sightseeing, shopping and going out to dinner every night.

Shawn returned home and we made an effort to solve our problems through counseling. Our pediatrician suggested a diet minus corn, wheat, and milk.

He said goat's milk would be good for him. I traveled several miles to purchase goat's milk from a farmer, but Shawn didn't like it very well. His depression lingered on and eventually we gave up on the diet.

When Shawn entered high school he made the track team and did quite well. He ran cross-country over ten miles a day. He seemed less depressed, and had a girlfriend. However, by Shawn's Junior year something was drastically wrong. While running for the track team he was riddled with fear and suffered panic attacks as he jogged along the highway. He was fully convinced fumes from passing cars were asphyxiating him. He refused to set foot on our sun deck—fearing the deck stain might harm him. He used paper towels to protect his hands when opening or closing doors, and lined the toilet seat with paper before using it. He angrily accused me of trying to poison his food with garlic. At times he concocted strange mixtures of flour and water which he ate. I had little patience with his antics and arguments.

Our home was in turmoil once again. I was at my wit's end with this child, but I continued to seek direction through prayer.

Chapter Seven

Family In Crisis

Gigi's roommate married and moved out of their apartment. Gigi was dating her new boss at the restaurant. He moved in.

She called me one evening in tears. "Mom, as long as I have this boyfriend and this job, I'll never be right with God. Can I quit my job and move back home?"

The next day I helped her move home.

She began praying about what to do with her life as she studied a catalogue from the local college. She felt sick and run down physically. Her mornings began with nausea and flu-like symptoms. I asked her if she might be pregnant. She admitted that it was possible. We purchased a pregnancy test at the drugstore.

On May eleventh, Mother's day, I heard a loud wail from her bedroom. "Noooooo!"

It could mean only one thing. The test was positive!

I held her in my arms as she cried. I assured her we'd stand behind her, whatever she decided to do. First of all, she needed to tell her ex-boyfriend.

*Mike wanted nothing to do with fatherhood, and offered to pay for an abortion.

Ted wanted to talk to Mike face-to-face, and they arranged to meet at a local coffee shop. Mike brought his stepfather along. The angry, bitter man counseled Mike to deny any responsibility, "It's probably not his anyway," he said. Mike said very little.

Ted came home and reported the results of the meeting. "It's plain to see, he doesn't care anything about her. She's better off without him."

Gigi was crushed and guilt ridden. "Oh Mom, this is the worst thing in the world for a Christian girl— I feel terrible! How could I let this happen?"

"We'll get through this too, let's pray."

We scheduled an appointment for crisis pregnancy counseling through a local Christian agency.

At the same time, Shawn's problems were escalating. The guidance counselor from his school requested a conference.

Ted and I met at the school where a student directed us to Mrs. Youngquist's office. Her warm smile put us at ease as she motioned to chairs opposite her desk. She told us Shawn's bizarre classroom behavior included not doing assignments, disrespect, throwing food, and hiding behind partitions. The counselor gave us the name of a therapist the school recommended. I called and made an appointment.

Shawn entered the psychologist's office under protest. He sulked as he slumped on a sofa—his arms tightly folded across his chest.

A slight, bearded man entered the room and greeted us with all the charm of a grave digger. His solemn demeanor intensified as he quizzed Shawn and jotted notes. He invited Shawn into his inner office for more questions and some tests.

I leafed through outdated magazines and pondered how different my life might have been without children. When they returned, the doctor directed his questions towards me. "Tell me, Mrs. Genengels, are you missing any of your underwear?"

"No... I don't think so."

He stroked his beard absently and furrowed his brows. He directed his gaze towards Shawn: "Shawn, do you ever wear your mother's underwear?"

"No! Do you?" Shawn snapped.

The doctor wasn't amused. He concluded that Shawn's problems stemmed from his religion. "Most likely he's having problems because he's confused about sex, that happens with Christians." His dark eyes narrowed as he addressed me: "Do you have hang-ups about sex? I mean—being a Christian?"

I thought a moment before answering. "Well, sex was God's idea. I don't have a problem with it."

The doctor then launched into a tirade about his troubled childhood. He admitted he once felt guilty about his sexual feelings due to his mother's religious beliefs.

"Do you believe in God?" I asked.

He sighed and whispered "No."

Shawn refused to go to the next appointment. He ran to the beach while I hollered at him to get in the car. I called the doctor's office and told the receptionist I couldn't get Shawn's cooperation. We were billed eighty-five dollars for the session.

I reported back to the school guidance counselor. She disputed the doctor's conclusion that Shawn's religion was the root of his problems. "Most of the kids I see are confused about sex at this age."

She suggested a psychiatrist, Doctor *Star. "Perhaps Shawn will relate better to him." It was several weeks before he had an opening. I scheduled an appointment.

On Sunday, May 18, 1980, Mt. St. Helen's blew her top, scattering ashes everywhere. I knew how she felt, I was about ready to blow mine too!

Ted's father showed up unexpectedly on our doorstep, announced that he had cancer and was moving in. He'd driven straight through from Illinois to Washington. His suitcases lined the hallway. The only place we had for him was in Shawn's room. Our house was in further chaos.

"Ted we have to get away—so we can talk in private," I said.

I picked an out-of-the-way restaurant where I thought no one would know us. We were waiting to be seated when one of Ted's co-workers greeted him with a hearty slap on the back. "Hey, good to see you man! Why don't you two join our family?"

Ted said, "Sure, sounds like fun!"

I was furious when he sat down next to his friend. I hardly said a word as we dined at a table with noisy toddlers flinging food everywhere. When we left the restaurant I began to cry. Through tears I blubbered,

"I feel like I'm being torn in every direction at once. I can't handle Gigi's pregnancy, Shawn's mental illness, and your dad's cancer. We've got to find another solution."

We prayed for wisdom. The answer came when Ted's father moved to an apartment complex for senior citizens. It was clean, affordable, comfortable, on the bus line, and near his doctor. We could still keep an eye on him, and he seemed much happier being in his own place.

Gigi weighed her options of keeping her baby, or placing it for adoption. A friend suggested she spend the next few months helping at an isolated retreat house. We took her to visit the facility. Afterwards she wept, "I guess you don't want me around to embarrass you any more."

I tried to reassure her. "I do want you with us, I just don't know what you want!". We dismissed the idea of the retreat house and Gigi remained at home with us.

As my health deteriorated I realized I must care for myself too. That meant learning how to say "No." When asked to supervise vacation Bible school, the Lord counseled me: *"Not this summer, Carol. Someone else will do it."*

A friend encouraged me to enroll Ryan in swimming lessons. Again, the Lord guided my path: *"No. Ryan will be all right."* (The following fall Ryan's entire third grade class participated in *Operation Drown Proof*—swimming and diving lessons.)

Things smoothed out and we began looking forward to the new arrival.

But Shawn's behavior puzzled me. While getting ready for school he closely inspected each item of clothing for anything with the slightest flaw or stain. His appearance had to be perfect, his shiny black hair combed just so. Though he obsessed on cleanliness, his room was a shambles. He tossed orange peels and apple cores on top of clothes, candy wrappers and school papers. Every so often I'd spend the day cleaning up his mess.

I was plagued with blinding migraines, and dreaded the psychedelic auras that preceded the tormenting headaches. Usually the relentless pounding triggered severe bouts of vomiting leaving me exhausted. No medication seemed to daunt the pain—I couldn't keep anything down anyway. Continued female problems required minor surgeries. God gave me strength when I didn't think I could continue on.

As my dependence on the Lord increased, my gratitude deepened. One of the ways God's love sustained me was through little Ryan. His childlike faith and insights never ceased to amaze me. He shared his faith openly and prayed without hesitation.

One morning Ryan asked, "Mama, are the colors of the rainbow Jesus' favorite colors or the fruits of heaven?"

"Maybe they are Jesus' favorite colors," I said.

Meanwhile, Shawn grudgingly agreed to see the psychiatrist who came highly recommended for his work with teenagers. After one session, the doctor diagnosed Shawn with schizophrenia and prescribed medication "designed to bring him into reality."

Shawn took the pills under protest, refusing them altogether after a few days. "Why don't you at least give them a chance?" I urged. "They're supposed to help you!"

"I just can't stand those pills Mom!" he cried.

"Why not?"

"I can't run when I take those things. They make me so tired. I feel like I'm in a coffin and can't get out!" The look of desperation in his blue eyes begged me to understand. Track was about the only thing that kept Shawn going to school, and running meant the world to him. I called the doctor to tell him how the medication affected Shawn.

"That just proves it's doing what I want it to do!" he said. "I'd like to admit him to a psychiatric hospital."

"A hospital?"

"Yes, with a hospital setting and medication I can get him exactly where I want him. Maybe then we can make some progress!"

He asked me to schedule an appointment for the next afternoon to further discuss hospitalization.

I called an emergency prayer session with Ann and Jane for the next morning. At Jane's dining room table the three of us claimed the scripture promise...*If any of you lack wisdom, let him ask of God, that giveth to all men liberally...But let him ask in faith, nothing wavering. For he that wavereth is like a wave of the sea driven with the wind and tossed. For let not that man think that he shall receive any thing of the Lord. A double minded man is unstable in all his ways* James 1:5-7 (KJV).

We prayed for wisdom and direction, as well as protection for Shawn. Peace settled over us as we continued to intercede. I left our prayer meeting with an assurance that Jesus would open or close the doors in Shawn's path.

Later that afternoon, Ted, Shawn and I settled into leather sofa cushions in the doctor's office. Impressive framed certificates graced the walls.

The doctor entered the room and sat opposite the three of us. The tall, balding man reiterated his plans for hospitalization.

Shawn glared in defiance. "I *will not* go to any dumb hospital!"

The doctor stood up. With a hand washing gesture he declared: "In that case... I wash my hands of this case entirely. I refuse to treat Shawn any further."

Ted pushed himself up from the sofa: "Fine, let's go!"

I guess this is our answer! I know Shawn's a handful, but washing your hands of a case after two visits?

Shawn heaved an audible sigh and sprinted towards the door. Ted and I followed behind him. We knew that this door was definitely closed.

(Months later the psychiatrist made the front page of the newspaper. Several patients had filed sexual misconduct suits against him. He was tried, found guilty and lost his license to practice. He left town in disgrace.)

Thank God that Shawn was spared any trauma from him.

I was beginning to feel like a truant student as I

returned to the school. The guidance counselor seemed genuinely concerned about Shawn, and sensitive to our plight. She suggested a medical doctor, one specializing in nutritional therapy.

Our next venture found us sitting in yet another office, answering more questions. Dr. *Cole. assured us he would do everything possible to get to the bottom of Shawn's problems. He ordered blood work, a hair sample and allergy tests. His assistant administered a battery of psychological tests.

Shawn related surprisingly well to his new doctor. The tests results showed Shawn's system to be severely depleted of vitamins and nutrients. His junk food diet included: Twinkies, fries, pizza, potato chips, candy bars, and soda pop. He often skipped breakfast because he wasn't hungry. The demands of running further stressed his body.

The therapist disagreed with the schizophrenia diagnosis. "I think he's as neurotic as hell though!" he said.

Shawn was placed on a sugar-free diet and megavitamin therapy. We lugged home several bottles of vitamins. Shawn was agreeable to following the diet and taking vitamins. I read labels, planned meals, and researched the effects of refined sugar on the body. I read the book *Sugar Blues* by William Dufty, and a lot of things began to add up. I made sure Shawn ate a balanced breakfast and carried nutritious snacks like fruit and nuts, as well as a good lunch.

Shawn soon settled down and began handing in assignments. He was feeling and acting much calmer. With the help of his guidance counselor he soon caught up with his classmates. He finished Driver's Ed, and earned a letter in cross-country track. Since he was making progress we agreed that he could try for his driver's license.

Ted bought an older car from a neighbor and got it running. Shawn now had wheels of his own. It was a great help getting to and from school at odd hours for track practice. Though Shawn improved academically, he was still rude and argumentative at times. After he exploded in an episode of verbal abuse towards me, Ted laid down the law, "Either you shape up and abide by our rules, or ship out!"

"Fine! I'm outta here!" Shawn said. He tossed a few belongings into his car and took off. Our home felt like a battleground for the hordes of hell that were out to destroy us. After a week of living in his car Shawn returned. "What were those rules?" he asked sheepishly.

I came across the book *I prayed, He Answered,* by William Vaswig. It's the story of a Lutheran pastor's mentally ill son who was healed through prayer. The Vaswig's had a healing ministry in a Seattle suburb. I made an appointment for Shawn.

Pastor Vaswig and his son welcomed us into their office. The father/son team spent a long time praying over Shawn. They rested their hands on his shoulders, and prayed quietly in the Spirit.

Shawn continued to improve. A family friend, Betty, offered him a summer job at a camp for handicapped individuals. Under her guidance, Shawn worked hard helping challenged campers eat and dress. He took them on walks, or pushed their wheelchairs. It was a time of growth as he learned to give of himself. His patience and compassion for these children and adults was remarkable.

* * * *

Gigi attended Aglow meetings with me where I served as president of the Bremerton chapter. As her pregnancy advanced and people began asking questions, I had to deal with my pride. *"Lord, this is embarrassing. People can see she's pregnant."*

The Lord answered very clearly. *"Carol, where else would you rather she be?"*

"Nowhere, Lord. Nowhere."

One day our family accompanied a group from our church to a Christian Festival. Various musicians and speakers were performing at different parts of a huge fairground. The youth group was listening to a concert. As Gigi listened to Danniebelle's anointed singing, she sensed strong, loving arms reaching towards her. She melted in His embrace as repentant tears flowed freely on a hot, summer afternoon.

The following weeks were spent preparing for the new arrival. I attended childbirth classes as Gigi's coach. It was humbling for both of us, but we made the best of it.

Friends from my Aglow chapter hosted a baby shower. Gigi learned a great deal about God's unconditional love from these women. The baby was due the first week in December. We hoped and prayed it wouldn't come while I was in Jerusalem.

Chapter Eight

Blessed

*A*glow was holding their international fall conference in Jerusalem, Israel. Ann and I learned
about it in early spring, but we promptly dismissed
the idea. We couldn't afford a trip like that! Besides,
with all the chaos going on in my home there was no
way I could leave. But, the Lord clearly spoke to me.
*"You haven't asked me. If I want you to go, I will pro-
vide for you. I will make a way where there seems to
be no way."*

Ann felt the promise was for her too, and we
prayed together for confirmation. My confirmation
came the next afternoon as I read my scripture for
the day, *Our feet shall stand within thy gates, O
Jerusalem* Psalm 122:2 (KJV).

Every dollar needed for our trip miraculously
trickled in over the next few months. My Aglow
chapter raised $650 with fund-raisers and dona-
tions. Friends handed me twenty dollars here, and

ten dollars there. Cashier's checks arrived in the mail. Our dilapidated old boat sold for over five hundred dollars. My dad gave me silver dollars to use as tips. Ann's money came in through various mysterious sources.

We collected numerous prayer requests to take to Jerusalem.

Gigi promised to look after the family while I was gone. My bags were packed and I was waiting for Jane to pick me up. She was going to drive Ann and me to the airport. I was giving Gigi last minute instructions ... "And please don't have that baby until I get back!" I said, patting her large tummy. We spent several minutes reflecting on God's faithfulness, marveling at how He'd met my every need.

Gigi's loving eyes sparkled: "Oh Mom—of all the women I know—you are really blessed, I'm so lucky to have you for my mom."

She shall rise up and call you blessed. With a grateful heart, I explained how her words fulfilled a promise. A promise given six years earlier—when I desperately needed it.

Ann and I waved good-bye to Jane before boarding the 747 bound for New York. From there we would fly to Amsterdam, and then travel on to Tel Aviv. After touring Israel we would spend a few days in Cairo Egypt before flying home.

Three weeks later I returned to a ***Welcome Home*** banner and a decorated cake. Gigi hadn't had the baby yet! That night the family listened intently as I recounted my adventures in the Holy Land. We worshipped in Jerusalem, Bethlehem, and on Mt. Carmel.

We swam in the Dead Sea, the river Jordan, and visited the Sea of Galilee. We visited the garden tomb, and numerous other holy sites. In Egypt we toured museums, rode a boat on the Nile, and climbed inside of pyramids. Ann and I experienced the trip of a lifetime, and Jesus had sent us there.

A week later, just after midnight, Gigi called to me: "Mom, I'm scared...my water broke, I'm not so sure I want to go through with this!"

"It's too late to back out now honey, you don't have much choice."

I did my best to reassure Gigi as I cautiously drove to the hospital over icy roads.

Gigi was admitted and taken to a labor room where we spent the night and all the next day. I was a lousy coach, I forgot everything from the childbirth classes as she suffered. "Just squeeze my hand honey," I said.

Later that afternoon, I had the honor of being present at the birth of my first grandchild.

"It's a boy!" the doctor said. Nathan was the chubbiest little newborn I'd ever seen.. The adorable baby with three chins was a wonderful, welcome addition to our family. While the doctor finished with the stitches, a nurse wheeled the infant next to Gigi. She reached over to stroke his hand, and his tiny fist grasped her finger.

"I love you little boy," Gigi said, as tears spilled from her hazel eyes.

* * * *

Though a Thousand fall...

Shawn made progress in his Senior year. He took classes at the Skill's Center where he learned to repair outboard motors, a hobby he enjoys to this day. He and his girlfriend attended a couple of dances. He continued with track.

Recruiters for the armed services came to the high school and a Navy recruiter called our home incessantly. One afternoon Shawn proudly announced his decision to join the Navy. He was scheduled to leave at the end of the summer following graduation.

I wasn't at all sure he was ready for the Navy, or that the Navy was ready for him. I worried about his fragile mental state, and feared he might crack under the pressure of boot camp. Nothing I said convinced him to reconsider his decision.

His big day finally arrived; I was about to drive him to meet the Navy bus. He tossed his duffel bag into the back seat of the car. His hair dryer was sticking out of the canvas bag.

"I don't think you'll be needing that, Shawn." I said.

"Why not?" he asked.

His cheeks grew pale as I explained: "One of the first things they'll do is sheer off your hair!" *He has so much to learn Lord, so much.*

I kissed Shawn good-bye and promised to write letters. I watched my first born son hoist his duffel bag, (minus the blow dryer) up the steps of the bus. He turned and waved good-bye. I don't think he saw the tears in my eyes.

Every day I begged God for a miracle for Shawn. Shortly after his arrival at boot camp we received a letter:

Dear Mom & Dad 10-08-81

I want out! I don't want out of the Navy, but I want out of boot camp. I'm beginning to hate it more and more. All I ever do is work hard and march most of the day. We must have a bunk made perfect, along with clothing folded step-by-step. If you have something wrong with these things when the inspectors come in, then you must go to a well disciplined exercise party. The "party" starts at about 8:00 PM and ends at ten at night. You must do 8 count body builders, leg stretches, raise legs and keep them up for 3-5 minutes and do it 3 times. You must do 100 jumping jacks, 25 push ups, sit ups, thigh bends, etc. ... I got my second uniform today which will be worn when I graduate in a little over 3 weeks from now. If I have to bust my bread loaves I will do it, because once I get out of boot camp and start my 4 week school then it won't be so bad. We must shave all the time prior to personal inspections. If we do not pass we go to exercise party, I shave so hard that my face bleeds, and sometimes I still don't have a proper shave.... I never get any phone-call breaks except once when nobody was home. I've been doing some praying lately because I think this is the hardest thing I have ever tried to accomplish. There are so many stupid rules one must follow and I get very little sleep at night. It's all very stressful, but I think

Jesus can help me and understands what I am going through. Our c/c is about the meanest, hardest c/c out of about 60 others. Sorry I can't write more, but have little time. I have to go already. Say Hi to Gigi, Ryan, and Grandpa. Love Shawn

Three days later we received another letter.

Oct. 11, 81 Dear Mom, Dad & Ryan;
I'm doing okay. I'm going into my service week this next week. This is where the recruits eat and do clean up, and food service. I got a letter from Aunt Sarah and was glad to hear from her. I'm really having a rather hard time here at boot camp. I try, but I sometimes make mistakes. I am always nervous... Maybe I am too negative, but I still can't seem to enjoy boot camp. I wish I were out. I get in trouble for the stupidest things. I'm trying to keep my temper from going crazy around this darn place. It gets hard when you live so close together with 70 other recruits and a mean commander. Sometimes we get on each others' nerves. I hope my family is doing okay. Are you? I love my family very much and will be praying for all of you. Love Shawn — I Love You

One morning, I was washing dishes when the Lord prompted me to drop everything and pray Psalm 91 over Shawn. I settled into my rocker, turned to Psalm 91, and began to pray.

"He who dwells in the shelter of the most high will rest in the shadow of the Almighty. You are his

fortress, his God in whom he trusts. Save him from the fowler's snare and from the deadly pestilence. Cover him with your feathers, let him find refuge under your wings. Let your faithfulness be his shield and rampart. Let him not fear the terror by night nor the arrow that flies by day, nor pestilence that stalks in the darkness, nor the plague that destroys at midday. Though a thousand fall at his side — let him stand.

I continued to intercede for three hours.

A week or so later I received a letter from Shawn. He had fallen asleep on watch and was sent to a special disciplinary unit. He had to make it there or he was out. The maneuvers were tougher than anything he'd experienced before. One blistering hot afternoon was the worst. Shawn and others loaded with heavy gear were forced to endure endless pushups and rigorous exercises. He was lying on his back holding his rifle over his head. Due to years of running and weight lifting his physical stamina was better than most.

Beads of sweat ran into his eyes as he sweltered in the heat. His head began to swirl as he struggled for breath. *"Help me Jesus, please!"* He heard the words: *"Praise Me Shawn."* As he began to praise God silently, his strength returned. He continued praising throughout the strenuous maneuvers meant to break him. Others around him were giving up. One man headed for the wall in an effort to escape. It was the closest thing to hell on earth that he had ever experienced. After the three hour ordeal he made it! His next letter brought us up to date.

Dear Family

I must tell you that I was in trouble a week or two ago. The company commander said I was in danger of being thrown out of the Navy on a discharge. I said to myself and the Lord that I must make it... For some reason God helped me to convince the RAB board that I was a sensible man and that I was capable of being in the navy. I was sent to a discipline unit and worked very hard. I got out at a surprisingly quick rate of time because I had passed another shore tour and got two perfect inspections. I then reported to my division officer after a week. He said he was happy with my performance and to forget the mistakes of the past. Love Shawn

Dear Mom, Dad & Ryan 11-5-81

I'm doing a lot better now because I did a good job on inspections, etc. I will graduate on November 13, 1981. I am very happy that I was able to get out of the special unit because a lot of people never seem to get out. One kid was there for 8 months. ...Soon I will be out of boot camp despite all my troubles and burdens. I am glad God helped me, and that I was not thrown out—like a lot of guys were. I will go to my 4 week school and then come home for Christmas on an airplane. I hope Dad's back gets better because I am praying for him. Love Shawn

(Shawn went on to serve six years in the Navy—seeing much of the world.)

The Lord watches over you, he is your shade at your right hand; the sun will not harm you by day, nor the moon by night. The Lord will keep you from all harm—he will watch over your life; the Lord will watch over your coming and going both now and forevermore, **Ps. 121:5-8 (NIV).**

* * * *

Gigi's baby brought much joy to our family, especially his uncle Ryan. Nathan was a placid baby with plenty of people to love him. Ted was a doting grandfather. Gigi proved to be a very attentive mother. When Nathan was three months old they moved to a place of their own. Though being a single mother was a challenge, Gigi did her best to make a cozy home for them. She was determined to put the mistakes of the past behind her and move on. On Sundays she bundled little Nathan up and pushed his stroller to the church on the corner. She joined a Bible study and made some new friends. She eventually met a wonderful guy who would become her future husband. Greg was crazy about little Nathan, as well as Gigi.

Gigi and I enjoyed a wonderful friendship and shared a mutual love for one another. We both cherished God's unfailing love that helped us through our difficult days. If only things were better with my mother. Our relationship left much to be desired. In order to understand the dynamics between us, we must travel back to my childhood. Please come with me back to when I was a little girl.

Chapter Nine

Come as a Child

January 1942-1954

T he rain on Seattle's hills froze the morning I was born. According to my parents, they were still reeling from the previous month's bombing of Pearl Harbor. They thought it was a terrible time to bring a new baby into the world.

Mom and Dad brought me home to Bremerton via ferry-boat. Unsightly, gray buildings and massive cranes dominated the banks of the snug harbor where the ferry docked. The Navy town burgeoned on the hills behind the naval shipyard and across the bay where our family lived in a housing project. My brothers, Paul and Chuckie, were waiting to meet me.

Mom could set her clocks by the shipyard whistle that announced the start of each shift. Dad worked as many shifts as he could tolerate. He and his co-workers were cautioned to: *"Button your lips, a slip of the lip might sink a ship*," as they toiled on the huge battleships moored in dry-dock.

I spent the first year of my life battling frequent bouts of pneumonia. Mom and Dad struggled to make ends meet while my medical bills piled up. With three young children the task must have seemed overwhelming.

Mom told me how she panicked one evening while bathing me. "Andy come quick!" She pointed to an angry red lump on my back—the size of an egg.

The family doctor cautioned my dad to hold me still while he siphoned the lump with a long needle. According to Dad, he shed as many tears as I did when my tiny eyes questioned: *Why do you let him hurt me Daddy?*

The doctor admitted that he didn't know what more to do, and referred us to a chest specialist in Seattle. I was promptly admitted to Swedish Hospital for the first in a series of hospitalizations.

Hospital beds overflowed during the war. At one point, the only place for me was in the hospital kitchen. One afternoon I reached through the metal rungs of my crib towards a shiny blade on a table. Mom was horrified when she visited and discovered my bandaged hand.

I've been told that times were especially tough as our family adjusted to the war rationing system. Mom used red stamps for meat and butter, and blue ones for canned goods and commodities. Mom and Dad's cigarettes were rationed too. Each family member was allowed three pairs of shoes in two years. If shoes wore out, the insides were lined with cardboard. Gasoline and tire rationing made carpools a necessity.

Tin cans, scrap metal, and even cooking fats, were taken to a collection site for war use. Mom subscribed to the war effort motto: *"Use it up, wear it out, make it do, or do without."*

The shipyard repair facility, a likely target, necessitated frightening air raid drills. At the sound of a siren, window shades came down and lights were switched off. Sinks and bathtubs were filled with water—to extinguish potential fires. The droning of planes brought an element of fear. Was it friend or foe?

President Franklin Roosevelt's radio broadcasts kept us updated on our military troops.

I was about three when a surgeon removed a rib from my back so tubes could be inserted to drain my lungs. Mom diligently changed the bandages between hospital visits, taking extra caution to spare me any unnecessary pain. I begged her not to take me back to the hospital, to no avail. I just couldn't understand why she left me in such a terrible place. I missed my mother the most at night when I cried for her.

One morning a white capped nurse urged me to climb aboard a gurney.

"No, I don't want to go to the operation room!" I protested.

"We're just going for a ride dear, it will be fun."

"I want my mommy, where is she?"

The nurse finally convinced me to climb onto my chariot. I was beginning to enjoy riding through the halls when I spotted familiar double doors. "No, no, take me back to my room!"

The determined nurse propelled the gurney through the frightful passage way. My eyes quickly surveyed the brightly lit room where doctors, nurses and trays of sharp, silver instruments stood waiting. I kicked and screamed as nurses transferred me to the operating table. My arms flailed in desperation as the sickening, damp ether mask clung to my cheeks. With a vengeance, I ripped the vile smelling thing away and flung it to the floor. My eyes sought a means of escape. The doctors swore as they helped pin down my arms and legs. Two hands placed the suffocating cloth back over my nose and mouth, holding it there until the circle of masked faces swirled away into darkness.

The days following surgery were a blur of nausea, pain, stitches, and the sting of adhesive tape being ripped from my skin.

Mom juggled her time between the boys and me, coping the best she knew how. We spent a lot of time at my grandparent's house on Capital Hill in Seattle. It was conveniently close to the hospital and my doctors. The Victorian house had lots of nooks and crannies to play in and a wonderful banister to slide down. Grandpa, a chiropractor, gave Mama frequent adjustments for her tension headaches.

I whiled away hours banging on their upright piano. Grandma confided that I was her "favorite," because I was named after her. She promised to give me the piano when I was older.

My colds and earaches lingered year round.

"Don't sniff, blow into this handkerchief!" my mother scolded as she placed steaming vapors by my bed so I could breathe. Mama chased me daily with a spoonful of cod-liver oil, which I detested. She crushed pills and put them into a teaspoon of jam. I can't lick a jam spoon to this day without tasting the gritty pills. She nursed my brothers and me through one thing after another; measles, mumps, whopping cough, chicken-pox and the flu. Her greatest fear was polio.

Mama was a great cook and there was always something wonderful baking in the oven. No one could resist her chocolate cakes, flaky pies and crunchy cookies. She made jams and jellies, sealing them with melted paraffin. A trellis of sweet-peas grew outside the kitchen window, and Mama often placed a glass jar with a colorful bouquet on the kitchen table.

I didn't like it when my parents yelled at each other. I'd hold a pillow over my head at night trying to block out their fights. When Mama cried, I'd run to her and push Daddy away so he wouldn't hit her any-more. I stayed by her side, patting her slim shoulders until she stopped crying and pulled me into her lap.

Mama smelled like Ivory soap and starch when she read to me. Weekly library trips kept us well stocked with new stories.

Following the war, a new wonder drug was released for civilian use. With penicillin my lung infections cleared up once and for all. No more oper-ations or hospitals!

I was about five when a neighbor invited me to attend summer Bible school. I didn't want to go. My brothers had warned me that school was a dreadful place. Though I protested, Mama made me go with the neighbor lady.

At Bible school I heard exciting stories told with paper dolls on a flannel-graph board. I learned that Jesus Christ isn't a swear word—He's a real person, the **Son of God.** He loves me so much that He died on a cross—*just for me*! Jesus gives presents like happiness, love and peace. *Do Mama and Daddy know about Jesus?*

I sang *Jesus Loves Me* and I could hardly wait to go back again the next day to learn more about Him.

I skipped up the sidewalk every evening to meet Daddy's bus on the corner. He'd pick me up and hug me tightly. "How's Daddy's best Girl?" Old Spice after-shave mingled with the aroma of Black Jack gum in his pocket. Sometimes it was Juicy Fruit. He'd offer me a stick (for after dinner) as we walked hand-in-hand down the hill.

I was seven when my baby sister was born. The day Sherry joined the family, I ran in from playing to get my first look at her. I raced upstairs where Mama was propped up in bed. She put her finger to her lips, "shush..." I tiptoed to the bassinet, and peeked in just as the baby spit-up. I began to cry. "Mama, baby Sherry doesn't like me!"

"What makes you say that?" Mama asked.

" 'Cause she took one look at me and threw-up!"

My baby sister took far too much of Mama's time and attention. Everybody fussed over the darling infant with dimples and blonde curls. I compared my brown bob in the mirror. "Straight-as-a-stick," that's what Mama always said. However, she beamed with pride when Sherry's picture won a prize in a pretty baby contest. Even Daddy spent too much time rocking that baby at night.

I decided to state my case. I folded my arms across my chest, and stomped my foot. "I'm jealous of baby Sherry!"

Mama yelled, "Shame on you, what a naughty, selfish girl you are. Jealous of a sweet, innocent baby!"

Mama cried a lot when Daddy and she fought. I felt sorry for Mama when she tried to hide her black eyes and bruises with make-up. It didn't do much good. After a fight, Mama usually took us kids to Grandma's for awhile.

Dad always begged Mom to come back home, promising he would never hit her again. They would eventually kiss and make up and things would settle down for awhile.

First Grade 1950

The cold wind penetrated my coat as I walked several blocks to my school. Most of the morning my first grade teacher vied with swirling snowflakes for the children's attention. As the storm intensified our teacher announced that school was being dismissed early. One-by-one mothers claimed their children and bundled them up for the walk home. I was the last child left. A lady I'd never seen before said she knew where I lived and offered to walk me home. She was wearing a bulky coat and a head scarf. She gripped my hand tightly and told me not to let go as we stepped outside into the blinding snowstorm. The stranger's hand guided me step-by-step through the howling blizzard. I couldn't see her face because I was totally engulfed in a white blur. Pelting flakes stung my eyes, cheeks, and frozen nose. I had no idea where we were, but I hung on for dear life. It seemed like ages before the lady released my hand at my doorstep and said, "Good-bye Carol," before disappearing into the storm.

Mama opened the door and hugged me tight, "I'm so glad you're okay!" She didn't know school had been dismissed early. We never did figure out who walked me home that day.

The next few days my brothers and I frolicked in the deep snow. We made snowmen and built igloos out of the drifts that sparkled like diamonds in the January sunshine. It was one of the worst snowstorms on record for the Pacific Northwest.

My second grade teacher, *Miss Lang, acted as if she hated children. She slapped us, yanked our hair, and yelled. One afternoon, as I day-dreamed at my desk, a heavy blow landed across my back, a bull's-eye! The searing pain to my scar took my breath away. Miss Lang snarled, "Get back to work, you lazy time waster!"

Tormenting nightmares haunted my sleep at night. Scary monsters waited patiently for me to close my eyes. My legs usually froze in place as a giant beast approached. One night I huddled in the dark after a terrifying dream. I was way too frightened to move or call for help. Then, in the fearful darkness, comforting words echoed from a far distant corner of my mind. *Jesus loves you. Jesus loves you.*

I cried out, "O Jesus, can you make my bad dreams go away? If you can, please help me." The plaguing nightmares ceased from that point on. I knew who had made them stop.

Sometimes Mama had bad dreams too. She was sick a lot. When she went to bed with a cold, headache, or cramps, Daddy would bring her a tray with food and a flower on it. He was nice to her when she was sick, but when Daddy was mean we could always go to Grandma's house, I liked it better there.

At Grandma's house I continued to pick out tunes on her piano. I'd sing along: *"Peter, Peter pumpkin eater, had a wife and couldn't keep her. He put her in a pumpkin shell, and there he kept her very well."* Grandma would smile at my love for the piano and remind me that it would someday belong to me. I imagined taking lessons and playing for my friends and family while they clapped.

Sometimes at Grandma's I wandered off by myself. One Sunday morning I heard music coming from a neighborhood church. I tiptoed up the steps and through the open doors. I slipped into a wooden pew in the back row and pretended the grownups sitting nearby were my family. Somehow I knew God's house was where I belonged. I so wished my mom and dad would go to church too.

* * * *

The Gift of Faith

When I was nine I rode the bus to downtown Bremerton all by myself. One day I wandered into the **Gospel Book Store** and picked up a bookmark with a curious verse: ***"Only one life, t'will soon be past; only what's done for Christ will last."***

I paid for the card, took it home, and tucked it away in my dresser drawer. The words lodged in my heart.

One evening I overheard my brother's friends arguing in the living room. Someone swore. Another guy said, "Hey! You shouldn't use God's name that way!"

The first voice said: "Aw, come on — you don't believe in God do you?"

As the debate continued my heart sank. *Is it all a lie, like Santa Claus?*

Saturday nights spent with my cousin, Linda, usually meant Sunday School the next morning at the Lutheran church on the corner. Though I had doubts about God, I liked being in the classroom that smelled like musty books and floor wax. One morning my teacher asked: "Carol, is something bothering you?"

I confessed that I wasn't so sure there was a God. She listened intently as I explained. "I just don't have any faith."

"Why don't you pray about that?" she suggested: "Just ask God to give you the gift of faith. I'll be praying for you too."

I took my teacher's advice to heart, praying

nightly before I went to sleep. *"Please God, give me the gift of faith."*

* * * *

When I was in the fourth grade our family moved to Silverdale. The small country town sported a couple of gas stations, a few taverns, and an equal number of churches.

My teacher at Silverdale Elementary seemed more like a grandmother than a teacher. My new friend, Janie, invited me to attend church with her on occasion. In summer we attended Bible classes at Silverdale Bible Church. One afternoon I was leaving the church to go home. As I started down the steps a lady called to me. "Carol—wait a minute, I want to ask you something."

I turned and looked up into glowing brown eyes. "What?"

"Have you ever asked Christ into your heart?"

"No," I answered honestly.

"Would you like to?"

"I guess so."

"First you must confess that you are a sinner, and that you need a Savior. Then ask Jesus to forgive your sins. I'll help—if you like."

As we prayed on the steps leading up to the church, Jesus entered a troubled little heart; a heart with much to learn about the *Most High God*—who chose to dwell there.

Now, one thing was certain. I *belonged* to Jesus.

At the end of the classes parents were invited to the closing program.

I stood straight and tall in front of the church while Mom looked on. Each class member had to recite a scripture from memory. Mine was John 3:16. *For God so loved the world, that he gave his only begotten Son, that whosoever believeth in him should not perish, but have everlasting life* (KJV).

I hoped Mom would be proud of me, but on the way home she ranted and raved about how mortified she'd been sitting amongst such dowdy women. "There I was—the only woman in the place wearing make-up and jewelry! I felt like Jezebel!"

I attended Sunday evening services with Janie as often as possible, but Mom was not pleased with my decision to worship with "a bunch of narrow minded fanatics."

Sometimes Dad gave me a ride to the Sunday evening services. But if he was too busy, I walked by myself. I was afraid in the dark, especially when barking dogs charged after me. It was then that I'd pray: "*Jesus... please take my hand.*"

Fear vanished into the night and dogs backed off when Jesus gripped my hand and personally escorted me to His house.

One day I prayed a heartfelt prayer: "*Jesus, when I grow up, please give me a husband who will take me to church.*"

* * * *

1954 —Age 12

One Sunday morning my parents had a surprise for my sister and me. We were going to Tacoma, an hour's drive away. Their plans included the zoo, lunch at a restaurant, and a movie. Sherry and I bubbled with excitement as we dressed for the trip.

After a fun morning spent exploring the zoo we returned to our car. Dad started the engine and we headed across town. The sunny day matched our moods as we rolled the windows down. Suddenly a car sped past ours sending gravel through the open window. A tiny chip lodged in my eye.

"Stop rubbing your eye," Mom cautioned, "you'll only make it worse!"

Dad parked in front of a drug store while Mom dashed in to buy some eyewash. She flushed my eye several times, but the rock wouldn't budge.

I pretended to be okay and we went on to the restaurant. I tried to hide my misery while eating my sandwich. Tears trickled down one side of my cheek as I dipped fries in ketchup. Dad suggested we skip the movie and go home.

"Noooo, please don't go home!" I begged, "I'm sure my eye will be better soon!"

I still remember bits of the Hitchcock thriller, *Rear Window*, starring James Stewart and Grace Kelly. Sherry followed me back and forth to the ladies' room as I splashed cold water into my eye. It hurt like crazy.

Finally, the movie ended and we headed for home. Mom tucked me into bed with a wet tea bag placed on my eyelid to soothe it.

I was still in considerable pain the next morning after a restless night. Mom let me stay home from school, but promised to come home from work on her lunch hour. She'd scheduled a noon doctor's appointment. I cringed at the notion of a doctor poking a needle in my eye, and spent most of the morning trying to figure a way to get out of the appointment.

Mom was due home within the hour, I was desperate! As I stared into the mirror, focusing on the tiny stone, I had an inspiration. *Maybe Jesus can help me!*

I cupped one hand beneath my eye and prayed. *"Jesus, will you please take this rock out of my eye?"*

At that precise moment the tiny chip popped into my hand. The relief was instantaneous. I could hardly contain my excitement as I called Mom and told her the good news. That afternoon the realization hit me. *I'm beginning to have faith! The very thing I prayed for!*

Chapter Ten

Teenage Years

The day I turned thirteen, my parents had a big fight and forgot my birthday. Though I loved my mother I was afraid of her. She was short tempered and angry much of the time. When she was really mad she yelled, "You're just like your father!" I never knew when she would lash out with a stinging slap across my face. The names she called me hurt the most. At least at school I had friends who liked me. Even a few boys. I fell in and out of love over the next few years.

I was sixteen when Grandma announced she was moving to an apartment. Finally, I was going to get the piano I'd dreamed of owning.

At last the big day arrived! Dad rented a truck and friends help move the instrument to our house. They struggled to maneuver the piano up concrete stairs, down the sidewalk, and into the house. Dad wheeled the cherry-wood upright into the living room and placed the bench in front of it.

My sister ran to the piano bench, sat down and began banging on the keys. She was as excited as I was.

"Mom, when can I start lessons?" I asked.

"You? Sherry's going to take piano lessons!" she said.

"Well, can I too?"

"Of course not! I can't afford to give both of you lessons. Besides— you're too old for piano lessons!"

"But it's *MY* piano!"

"That's just too bad! Life is full of disappointments, of all people—I should know! The sooner you realize that fact, the better." There was a chilling finality to her words, along with a menacing look in her eyes that I knew all too well.

I could hardly stand hearing my sister practice her lessons. It was all I could do to keep from crying at her first recital, the only one I ever attended.

Mom's attitude towards me was puzzling. Sometimes she was loving, but at other times she seemed to despise me. I observed three basic personalities. She was either the life of the party, sick and helpless, or mean and critical. Our lives revolved around her moods. Sometimes when she fought with my dad she would threaten to swallow a handful of pills. I was afraid she would do it. Our linen closet was well stocked with numerous prescription bottles. We could never plan ahead. Everything depended on how she felt at the last minute. As long as I could remember she'd been ailing, and when she wasn't sick she reminisced about the times she was. Every headache, cramp, cold, dental appointment, and physical twinge became a major lament that we were subjected to hearing every detail of.

I tried to please her but usually failed. It was my responsibility to clean house, do laundry, start dinner, do the dishes and keep an eye on my sister. I wasn't given an allowance. Baby sitting for others was my only source of spending money. Mom often volunteered me to sit free for her friends.

At the beginning of my sophomore year I made a new friend, Taffy. Her bedroom walls were plastered with as many Elvis pictures as mine. We listened to Top 50 songs on Seattle radio stations and watched *American Bandstand* to keep up with the latest music trends. Taffy and I attended a taping of *Seattle Bandstand*, a take-off of *American Bandstand*. I was chosen to be on a panel of judges for new records.

I was so excited about being on television that I gathered my whole family around the TV to watch the show. I wanted Mom to think I was wonderful, that I looked good on television, and that she was proud. Her only comment was, "How come you always have your mouth hanging open? It looks stupid."

Taffy and I spent hours rollicking with laughter at each other's antics. We often floated around the bay in a row boat, listening to music on her portable radio. We had another close friend, Elaine.

In summer we'd sleep beneath the stars in Taffy's back yard, confiding our hopes, dreams and plans for our future. We turned out for school plays, rooted in pep rallies, triple dated, and went to school dances together.

I was seventeen when Elaine and I decided to visit the newly built Silverdale Lutheran Church. I was impressed by the beautiful building with arched ceilings and stained glass windows. There was a sense of mystery in the liturgy. Elaine remained in the pew while I went forward to take communion. When I returned to my seat, Elaine whispered, "You shouldn't have done that!"

"Why not?" I gasped.

"You have to be a member to take communion." I looked around to see if everyone was staring at me. Nobody seemed to notice, except Elaine. *Maybe I'd better see about becoming a member.*

Elaine and I talked it over and decided we'd both like to join the church. We made arrangements with the minister to attend membership classes. We also joined the youth group, *Luther League.*

Elaine and I giggled our way through the classes as we struggled to understand Pastor Randoy's thick Norwegian accent. We were finally ready to be received into membership, but there was one problem—neither of us had been baptized.

Our baptism was scheduled for the evening prior to confirmation Sunday. We were encouraged to invite our relatives to the ceremony. My mom and dad had a party to attend and couldn't make it. Elaine's family sat behind the somber elders near the front of the dimly lit church. Elaine and I knelt at the altar. We tried not to giggle as Pastor Randoy sprinkled our heads with water and prayed over us.

Mom and Dad didn't come to church for my confirmation the next morning either.

Chapter Eleven

True Love

*E*laine and I shared a passion for roller skating. Friday evenings often found us lacing our skates to the sound of blaring organ music and wheels spinning on hardwood floors. I did a double take as a handsome fellow soared past us. The music stopped as the *All Skate* ended. Over the loud speaker a man's hollow voice announced: "The next skate will be a *Trio*."

"Come on Elaine, let's go ask that guy in the stripped shirt to skate with us."

Just then, someone tapped me on the shoulder. I spun around, it was him! "Would you girls skate the trio with me?"

The music began and the three of us joined hands. Ted was in the middle as we skated around the rink. He talked to Elaine most of the time. I assumed he wasn't interested in me, but he asked me to skate the next skate, a *Couple's Only*. Ted was a good skater. I learned he had moved here from Chicago, and was serving a machinist apprentice in the shipyard, as well as attending Olympic College. His hazel eyes twinkled more green than brown. He had thick wavy brown hair, a strong square jaw, and sensuous lips.

We skated together the rest of the evening. Though I liked Ted, I refused to give him my phone number. Later, I kind of wished I had as Elaine and I sat in her bedroom discussing our evening. "I think he really likes you! *Carol Genengels*, what a funny name that would be."

"I'll probably never see him again," I giggled.

A few weeks later we ran into him at the county fair. Ted and his friend, Skip, tagged after us all afternoon. When we left the fairgrounds they followed Elaine's car all the way to my house. We invited them in for a Coke. I was busy fixing snacks when Ted copied my number off of the phone. That evening we had our first date—bowling with Skip and Elaine.

When I learned that Ted was a Lutheran too, I invited him to church with me on Sunday, and home afterwards for a pancake breakfast.

Mom wasn't impressed with Ted. "I think he looks like a fish," she said.

Ted and I attended church together most Sundays. I loved hearing him sing hymns in his rich tenor voice. We enjoyed skating and bowling. He was a wonderful dancer and we instinctively sensed each other's moves on the dance floor. A huge silver ball splashed light around the room as we danced cheek-to-cheek. We dated weekends, and studied together week nights. We talked endlessly getting to know one another. Ted filled me in on his family background.

He confided that his mother was a patient at a state psychiatric hospital when his baby sister died of pneumonia. Ted's father did the best he could to care for his two sons, but they often had to fend for themselves; at times eating only bread and diluted condensed milk. The nearest school was a Lutheran parochial school. The little school gave Ted a scriptural grounding and a solid education until he entered public school in the ninth grade. He'd worked since he was old enough to cart papers—laboring in factories, on golf courses, and in grocery stores. He saved enough money to buy the saxophone he played in the school band. He paid for his own car and clothes. He lettered in football and graduated third in his high school class, earning a scholarship to Roosevelt University in Chicago. After his first year of college his dad sold the family home and encouraged Ted to move to Oregon with him. Ted had dreams of moving west someday, and agreed to go with his father and brother.

He helped his dad run a small general store in central Oregon. About a year later his dad tired of the venture and returned to Illinois.

Through an employment agency Ted learned of an apprenticeship in Bremerton Washington. He was a year into his machinist apprenticeship when we met.

I shared my dreams of being a fashion model, or

an airline stewardess, and my love of art and books. I wanted more education too, but most of all I wanted to get out from under Mom and Dad.

I was falling head-over-heels for Ted. He was cute, funny, intelligent, had goals, and faith in God. We began talking of marriage. We knew it would be tough financially, but figured we could manage somehow. On New Year's Eve he proposed. He couldn't afford an engagement ring, but I didn't care. We decided to marry as soon as I graduated from high school.

I turned eighteen at the end of January. Ted and I continued to talk of marriage for the next two months.

One night Ted telephoned in a panic. "I've got to see you right away."

I ran out to Ted's car when he arrived and looked deep into troubled hazel eyes. He stated, "I've been drafted! It looks like I have to go in the Army."

"The Army!" I cried. "What about college and us?"

"I don't know. I've got to report for some tests."

He learned the results of the tests a few weeks later. The recruiter said Ted scored higher than anyone from this county ever had. We prayed that he could get a deferment, since he worked for the government, and attended college.

I had news for Ted too. I was pregnant. We weren't proud of the fact that we had not waited until marriage. We prayed together, asking God's forgiveness, and decided we'd better cool it and set a date for our wedding. I dreaded telling Mom and Dad. Dad was living in Seattle managing an apartment complex. Mom planned to join him when the school year ended.

Mom learned I was pregnant from the family doctor. Her eyes flashed fire as she paced back and forth: "You disgust me! How could you be so unchaste? And how could you disgrace me like this? What ever will people think?"

She discharged a barrage of vile accusations of sleeping with every boy I'd ever dated. She had choice words for Ted too. Every evening, when she came home from work, she started in again with a vengeance. Though I usually had dinner ready, the table set, and the house clean, she never noticed. The obscene names she heaped on me were far more painful than the slaps in the face she usually gave me. I felt such guilt, shame and remorse. How I wished she'd take me in her arms and tell me that everything would be okay. It did not happen.

After dinner one evening my mother sat me down. She removed a small bag from her purse and emptied its contents into her hand. There was a hard, steely glint in her eyes. "Take this!" she ordered. Her outstretched palm contained a round black pill about the size of a marble.

"What's that?" I asked, my heart pounding.

"It'll take care of the pregnancy."

I stared in disbelief. "You mean it'll make me lose my baby? Where did you get that thing?"

"From the pharmacist," she said, "Don't worry it'll do the trick. You're only eighteen, you have your whole life ahead of you. There's plenty of time for babies later on." She rolled the miniature bowling ball towards me. "Now take this and be done with it!"

"But...I can't do that... I..I love this child!"

"That's crazy!" she said, "I never felt love for any of mine before they were born."

"Well I do! Ted and I are getting married!"

"Yeah, I'm sure *he* wants a kid. I'm telling you, he's absolutely no good! You'll be sorry if you marry him. He'll never amount to anything. Mark my words! You'll have nothing!"

"We will too—he's smart!"

She swore a blue streak. "I don't know what you see in that jerk! It'll never work out, never!"

"I love him and he loves me. I'm not going to take any pill!"

"You always were the stupidest girl in all the world! If you had a brain in your head you'd listen to me."

I ran to my room and cried myself to sleep, but I did not take the pill.

A few days later Ted came to see me. We left the house and went for a ride. I told him what my mother wanted me to do. A song came on the radio. "*The saddest words from tongue or pen, are these four words 'it might have been.'* "

"Let's get married as soon as we can, we'll figure a way," Ted said, as he dried my tears with his handkerchief.

We went to see the pastor of my church. Ted and I wanted God's blessing on our union. We were willing to be married in his study if necessary. Pastor Randoy asked us several questions, *but not the one we dreaded*. He checked his calendar and said he could marry us in May, six weeks away. He told me to contact the wedding coordinator. Since I was a member there would be no charge for the church, only the janitor's fee.

Mom had a fit when I told her we had made arrangements for a small wedding. "How am I supposed to plan a wedding on such short notice?" she screamed.

"We'll plan it," I said.

I asked Taffy and Elaine, to be my bridesmaids. I told no one, not even my closest friends, that I was pregnant. It would remain a secret as long as possible. I told people we moved our wedding date up because my mother wanted to move to Seattle, which was partly true.

"Mom, when can we shop for my wedding dress?" I asked.

"Are you out of your mind? I can't afford a wedding dress," she wailed. "Wear something you already have."

I was crushed. All I had was a couple of taffeta dresses, and a strapless formal, hardly appropriate for a wedding. I suggested perhaps my sister-in-law might let me borrow her wedding gown, as we were about the same size.

"There is no way in the world that she would loan her lovely dress to you!" Mom said. "Besides, you don't deserve a wedding dress!"

I wanted to be a beautiful bride for my handsome groom. I could see this wasn't going to be easy.

Mother did order wedding invitations from a local printer, but she said if we wanted flowers Ted could buy them. There would be no photographer either; that was an unnecessary expense. I could have only one bridesmaid. Ted could also pay the janitor's fee. Mom said she couldn't afford any of the things it took to put on a wedding. I felt so guilty. Dad was in Seattle and out of the picture. I had no one to turn to. *No one, except God!*

Taffy and I decided we'd better look for dresses as the wedding date was drawing near. She couldn't believe my mom wouldn't buy me a wedding dress. I'd saved all of my baby sitting wages and hoped it would do. We went downtown to an Anita store, known for fashionable clothes at reasonable prices. We began searching through racks of dresses.

I gasped. "Taffy look at this!" I stared at a white lace dress. It had a scooped neckline, three quarter length sleeves, and a fully lined ballerina-length skirt. A white satin sash with a center bow circled the waist.

"It looks just like a wedding dress!" I said.

"Wow, that is nice." Taffy said.

"Look, it's only seven dollars!"

A few hangers down, Taffy found an identically styled dress in a translucent nylon. The pastel floral print was perfect for a bridesmaid. It was six dollars! Our dresses fit perfectly. I felt like dancing around the store as we paid for our purchases.

"Aren't those dresses nice?" the sales clerk asked, "we just got those in."

When I showed my dress to Mom she was a bit irritated. But I didn't care, I was going to wear my dress with pride. I just wished she could have been happy for me.

The weekend before the wedding my brother and his wife came for a visit. When I proudly showed my dress to my sister-in-law she offered to let me borrow her wedding veil. I was thrilled.

Eventually the plans for our budget wedding came together.

The morning of my wedding my mother gave me instructions to finish cleaning the house for the company that was expected. She had to work and was not happy. "Why on earth did you have to plan a wedding for the drugstore's busiest day? The day before Mother's Day!"

That afternoon Ted and I delivered the cake and mints to the church. Some ladies were setting up the reception hall. One of them asked, "What kind of flowers are you going to decorate with?"

"We aren't having flowers," I informed her.

The women looked curiously at one another. Another lady said: "Do you have any flowers growing in your yard?"

"Well... yes—lots of lilacs, and we have a huge mock-orange bush full of white blossoms," I said.

"Lilacs and mock-orange would be perfect, can you bring a bunch in? We'll arrange them for you."

"Oh, yes!" I said, "that would be wonderful!"

Later, Ted and I delivered armloads of fresh cut blossoms to the church. Those wonderful women arranged fragrant bouquets for the sanctuary and reception hall. Someone had provided candles too.

That evening I tingled with excitement as I finished dressing at the church. Taffy helped me adjust my veil. I admired myself in a full length mirror. Ted had given me a small bouquet of white roses to carry on top of a white Bible.

I ascended the steps at the back of the church and stood next to my dad. Mom started to cry. "You look so lovely—I'm sorry dear, I only—"

"Not here, not now!" Dad scolded, "You'll have her in tears."

Mom's endeavor didn't go unnoticed. I wanted to hug her, but didn't. My brother ushered her to the front of the church next to Grandma and my aunts.

Elaine and my sister lit candles while an unknown soloist sang *O Perfect Love.*

Taffy preceded me down the aisle. Pale shafts of evening sunlight filtered through stained glass windows. I grasped my father's arm as the wedding march began. My beaming groom had never looked more handsome. My heart swelled with so much love and joy. I could hardly believe my good fortune.

Pastor Randoy stepped forward: "Who gifs dis voman to be married to dis man?"

"I do," my father said.

Pastor Randoy instructed us to use our full names. Ted began: "I Theodore Frederick, take thee Carol Livian, to be my lawfully wedded wife — for better, or for worse, for richer—for poorer, in sickness and in health, to love and to cherish, till death do us part."

I suppressed a giggle as I pledged to take *Theodore Frederick* as my wedded husband, and to live according to God's holy ordinance. We exchanged rings and knelt for prayer. The soloist sang

The Lord's Prayer before Pastor Randoy pronounced us husband and wife. "You can kiss da bride now," he said.

Ted lifted my veil, planted a kiss on my lips, and pulled the veil back down over my face. "You're supposed to push it back!" I whispered. He quickly complied. We linked arms and walked down the aisle to the organ recessional.

Our reception was brief and sweet. The best man took pictures with Ted's movie camera as we cut our wedding cake and fed each other bites. Our guests congratulated us one by one, and our opened wedding gifts were on display. I felt a surge of pride when a friend addressed me as "Mrs. Genengels."

We took a brief honeymoon trip to Olympic National Park. I had classes on Monday and Ted had work. We were planning an official honeymoon train trip in July. I adored my new husband, and he loved me.

Three weeks later, I wore my white lace dress beneath my graduation robe. Ted and my relatives watched me walk down another aisle to receive my diploma. Afterwards we returned to the house with the family. I felt a joyous pride of accomplishment before Mom's words shattered the moment. "Boy am I ever glad that's over. I've never sat through anything so boring in all my life!"

The next day Mom told me to sell my piano. She was moving to Seattle and a friend of hers had offered to buy it for fifty dollars. There was nothing I could do about it, I had no place to store it.

Chapter Twelve

Honeymooners

My husband and I moved our meager belongings to a tiny apartment in downtown Bremerton. We were overjoyed when Ted received a deferment from the Army because we were married. I'd never felt so completely loved by anyone before. Ted appreciated everything I did for him and didn't criticize me. I was determined to be the best wife possible. Cooking and cleaning for only two people was a breeze.

In July, Ted and I boarded the *Milwaukee Road* in Seattle, bound for Wisconsin. We spent most of the train trip cuddled in each other's arms. One morning the porter asked: "Well now, how are the newlyweds today?" When I asked how he could tell we were newlyweds, he just chuckled and shook his head from side to side.

I was fascinated by the majestic scenery as our train climbed and tunneled through mountain passes.

Ted and I relished gourmet meals in an elegant dining car. Crisp white linen cloths complimented fine china and sterling silver. Our cheerful waiter expertly followed the motion of the train as he poured beverage streams into our cups. We savored rich desserts, and planned our future as the train rolled through the picturesque countryside. Ted's father met us at the train station in Milwaukee and drove us to Illinois to meet Ted's brother Tim.

In Chicago Ted introduced me to the rest of his relatives and we explored the city. We spent hours at the Chicago Art Institute on Michigan Avenue. I was captivated by the Old Masters' paintings, the Picasso's, and the American artwork. My favorite painting was Edward Hopper's, *Nighthawks,* a 1942 oil painting of late night coffee drinkers in a diner.

One evening I nearly fainted at the Edgewater Hotel. We were seated at a table next to the stage when Frankie Avalon leaned towards me and crooned *"Oh Venus."*

Ted pointed out Wrigley Field where he and his dad used to attend Cub's baseball games. As we visited Chicago's parks, we puzzled over the fact that Lincoln's statue is located in Grant Park, and Grant's statue is in Lincoln Park.

We visited Ted's mother at Elgin State Hospital. She was overjoyed to see us. I was curious as to why she had to stay in a mental institution. She seemed sweet and pretty normal to me; she obviously adored Ted. She confided how she still mourned the death of her little daughter, and hoped we would have a baby girl. I promised to write and send pictures when our baby was born.

Ted and his dad took turns driving as we headed back to Seattle in Lambert's car. I spent most of the trip reclining on the back seat reading magazines—with my feet stretched out an open window in the scorching summer heat.

The cool air of western Washington embraced us like an old friend as we reached home. We took Lambert to meet my folks. Dad liked him, but Mom let it be known that she didn't care for him at all. I wasn't surprised.

Five months later my dad came to visit me the day I was scheduled to enter the hospital for my baby's birth. I told him I was frightened, and how I hoped Mom would come to see me when the baby was born. He said he didn't think she would come. Her last words had been: "You made your bed—now lie in it!"

Dad hugged and kissed me good-bye in the pale November sunshine before boarding the ferry back to Seattle.

That evening I was admitted to the hospital and prepared for the big event. After laboring all night in a room all by myself, (husbands weren't allowed in the labor room) I was sure I was close to death when the doctor arrived. He gave me an injection and I relaxed as it took effect. "Push, push!" he ordered. As I watched in the overhead mirror a baby's head emerged. In a matter of seconds my bulging stomach disappeared and a crying infant was placed on top of me. "It's a girl!"

"She's so tiny." I said. "Is she okay?"

The doctor laughed heartily. "I'd say she's a good seven pounds!"

I stared in wonder at God's gift to us. She was absolutely beautiful, even with her wrinkled, red face. She had perfect little fingers and toes. Her tiny tongue wet her lips.

After the doctor finished my stitches a nurse wheeled me into the hallway. I cuddled Gigi close to me as we lay on the gurney. I was overjoyed to finally see my husband walking towards us. He kissed me and stared at the miniature bundle in my arms. He was allowed to hold his daughter for a few minutes before being asked to leave. I cradled Gigi close as he slowly walked away. He turned around and looked longingly at his new little family.

Friends and neighbors brought flowers and gifts, but there was no word from my parents. Ted had called them right after Gigi's birth to tell them they had a granddaughter. Though they lived only a ferry ride away, they chose not to come.

I hugged Gigi close as Ted drove us home from the hospital. He parked the car in our driveway, got out and opened my door. I handed him the baby and he disappeared into the house. I finally realized he was not coming back for me. I limped into the house and went to our bedroom. I found Ted sitting on the edge of the bed beaming at the little doll nestled in his arms.

I was bewildered as to what to do with my new baby. I'd studied books on child care, but I needed my mother. I remembered how Grandma stayed with our family when my sister was born and many times when Mom was sick. I called from a pay phone to tell my mother how precious Gigi was, and invited her to come and see us. I confessed that I was afraid I might drop her.

Mom laughed and assured me that Gigi wouldn't break. "You'll learn like every other mother has. I'm too busy to come and see you." I felt such pain and rejection.

I listened to election returns of President Kennedy while I nursed my baby. The future First Lady was expecting a new baby any day.

Ted's mother sent a small package with a card. I unwrapped a knitted baby bonnet and booties along with three dollars—all the money she had. She was thrilled that we had a girl. I sent pictures and promised to keep her informed of Gigi's progress.

Gigi was three weeks old when we took her to Seattle on Thanksgiving to meet her grandparents. Mother's attitude seemed to soften a little when she saw her beautiful first granddaughter. However, she didn't waste any time criticizing the way Ted handled his new baby.

Chapter Thirteen

School Daze

1962-1966

*I*n June of 1962, Ted proudly waved his apprenticeship certificate. He was officially a journeyman machinist. It was time to go on to the university. I was expecting another child. When I was five months pregnant we were involved in a rollover auto accident. I flew out of the door and ended up sitting on the ground next to the car. The car was totaled but miraculously we all escaped without a scratch. The accident left me quite shaken emotionally though. We had to dip into our savings to buy another car, and that meant postponing Ted's education another year.

Our son Shawn was born in October during the Cuban missile crisis. Our future seemed uncertain as America teetered on the brink of war.

The doctor carefully unwound the cord from around the baby's neck. Shawn was the most beautiful baby I'd ever seen—with jet black hair, blue eyes, and long dark lashes. We were overjoyed with our tiny son.

My parents didn't come when he was born either. Mom still harbored bitterness towards Ted. She couldn't see that he was a good husband and father. He worked hard to support us, and took his little family to church faithfully. My childhood prayer for a man to take me to church had surely been answered.

Finally, in the fall of 1963, we moved to Seattle. Ted entered the University of Washington school of engineering. We saw more of my parents and they eventually warmed up to their grandchildren.

Even though times were very tough financially, Ted and I were secure in our love. But I lived on an emotional roller coaster where Mom was concerned. Whenever I thought things might be getting better with her, she'd stir up trouble between my siblings and me, playing us against each other. When my sister-in-law told me the things that my mother said about me and Ted it tore at my heart. At other times her openly, caustic criticism of Ted caused deep wounds to my soul.

I didn't know where to get help for my battered emotions and I wearied close friends with my laments. It seems strange now, but the more my mother put me down the harder I tried to please her. I'd do almost anything to win her love and approval. I gave her gifts that I thought she would like but they were never good enough. She'd point out something wrong with them. One year I splurged and bought her a beautiful lingerie set, a gown and matching robe. Her only comment was, "I'd freeze to death if

I wore that thing."

Mom constantly misread my motives and accused my sister-in-law and me of laughing at her when we were doing nothing of the kind.

I couldn't understand her. She'd been good to me when I was a sick little girl.

I lacked confidence. One afternoon I went to pick up the kids from my neighbor's house. I apologized for being late and made some disparaging remark about myself.

My neighbor asked: "Carol, why do you always put yourself down like that?"

"I guess I do it before someone else can."

"You really should stop it," she advised. "It only makes you look stupid."

I was embarrassed by her remarks, but I knew she was right.

However, it would be a long time before I would take steps to deal with the pain that I felt everyday.

Ted's senior year was the hardest. He was grieving the death of his mother, working part time, and constantly studying. One evening he did not return home with the car pool. A nurse called from the university hospital. Ted had collapsed on campus with blood streaming from his nose and mouth.

A neighbor took me to the hospital. The sight of tubes coming out of him scared me so—I stood frozen in the doorway crying and praying.

Studying all night, attending classes, and working in the campus machine shop was too much. Ted had bleeding ulcers. The doctor asked if he was under any stress, and warned that some life-style changes were in order. "No one can burn the candle at both ends all the time and expect to keep going!" The doctors froze the ulcers with a solution and Ted was able to eat a regular diet the next day.

My beloved grandmother died in January. After her death I wrote a letter to the lady who had bought my piano. I explained how much the piano meant to me, and asked her to let me know if she ever decided to sell it. She answered my letter saying I could buy the piano back for the same price she paid, fifty dollars. I was overjoyed the day that Ted borrowed a truck and moved it to our home.

No one was happier than I on Ted's graduation day. He looked so handsome in his cap and gown as he went forward to claim his bachelor's degree in mechanical engineering. His smile matched mine as we hugged.

We'd reached a milestone. Though Ted had several job offers, he decided to work for Boeing Airplane Company in Seattle.

We bought our first home in Redmond — a suburb of Seattle. The new split-level sat on a corner lot surrounded by mature evergreens.

After we were settled I proudly showed Mom around our new home. As we stood in the living room, her eyes took on that callous, steely glint. "Hmmh, two fireplaces!" She snapped, "I never even had one!"

Why can't she ever be happy for me?

Mom glared at my piano in the recreation room. "I should have had that piano," she declared. "I don't know why Mama didn't give it to me!"

New Horizons - 1968-74

I had just come in from weeding my flower beds when I learned Robert Kennedy had been shot and killed in Los Angeles. Two months prior to that, civil rights leader, Martin Luther King Jr., had been slain. Horrific scenes of the Vietnam war invaded our living room nightly, via the television. There was unrest in the White House. I was disillusioned with America and depressed.

Ted was offered a job in Pittsburgh and we decided to pursue it. The job, a wonderful opportunity, proved to be all consuming and a major adjustment for our family. We did get to see a lot of the east on our vacations. Gigi was often sick and spent some time in Pittsburgh's Children's hospital. After two years we moved back to Bremerton where Ted resumed working for the federal government.

We spent each weekend house hunting. I scanned the newspaper's real estate section daily. An ad caught my eye. *"Bungalow on 100 feet of waterfront, spectacular view."* The following Saturday morning we drove to Seabeck, turned down a steep gravel driveway, and pulled up in front of a Cape Cod style house. The musty old house with water stained ceilings needed a lot of work. I pictured the difference paint and a lot of elbow grease would make.

The view from the bay windows was breathtaking. Snowcapped Olympic mountains loomed majestically behind a curved bay of salt water. We went outside and carefully made our way down rickety steps to the beach at low tide. A potent iodine and seaweed scent permeated the gentle breeze. The kids shrieked as clams spit on their shoes. We gingerly dodged barnacles on the oyster laden beach. Wild roses and blackberries grew along the bank.

We fell in love with it, put down earnest money, and signed papers to buy the house. By the time we moved to Seabeck I was fighting morning sickness. Ted was beginning to think there was something about the air in Bremerton. We were overjoyed at the prospect of a new baby.

Our son, Ryan, born in December, was the cutest baby in the nursery with dark blonde hair, blue eyes, and a cupid's bow mouth. We brought him home and placed his infant seat beneath the Christmas tree with the rest of the gifts. Ted had his camera ready as I placed a big bow on the baby's head.

My parents came to visit on Christmas day in the middle of a snowstorm. Mom was finally beginning to accept Ted, and baby Ryan quickly won her heart. He was a placid, happy infant.

Ted's job was demanding, and finances were tight again. Gigi was usually sick, and Shawn still had raging headaches. Even though I had a new baby I adored, I was depressed. There seemed to be a void in me that nothing could fill. My days consisted of fixing up the place, and running the kids to the doctor.

In 1973, my parents moved back to Silverdale to fix up the old homestead. My relationship with my mother improved slightly, but she was still extremely critical of me personally. One evening while they were visiting I learned the real reason for her resentment. Mom was on the warpath as she screeched, "It took us years to pay off all of your blasted hospital bills. Your father and I would have been much better off if it hadn't been for you!"

"Why didn't you just let me die then!" I wailed.

"Maybe we should have!" She countered back. "Come on Andy, let's get out of here!" My dad looked sick as he turned and followed her out of the room.

Whenever we argued my mother gave me the silent treatment for weeks to come. My efforts to make peace were ignored until her anger fully subsided.

I don't know how I would have survived the next few years, had I not found Jesus when I did.

Chapter Fourteen

Growing in Christ

1983-1995

*I*n January of 1983, Gigi married her fiancé, Greg, in the same church that Ted and I married in. Shawn was in the Navy stationed in Guam, and Ryan was a happy, healthy eleven-year-old.

That spring I underwent a hysterectomy for a pre-cancerous condition. During surgery a mass was discovered near my liver and pancreas. Another operation would be necessary as soon as the present site healed. My doctor prepared me for the worst, pancreatic cancer. I sought the Lord in prayer like never before.

In August I entered surgery, a second time, trusting I was in God's hands. As I awoke from the anesthetic I heard the doctor's voice. "You're a very lucky lady, the mass was only a benign cyst on your liver. You should be as good as new in a few weeks."

In September Mom and Dad were planning their 50th wedding anniversary celebration. They rented a banquet room and sent out invitations. I arrived early to help decorate and greet the guests. Mom and Dad were late. Finally, Mom swirled through the door in her pink floor-length ball gown, looking every bit the party queen. Dad and my siblings followed close behind. My brother carried a carton of corsages, but there was one problem. My mother "forgot" to order a flower for me. There were carnations for her, my sister, and both sisters-in-law. She brought a leftover dog-eared, silk corsage for me to wear. I couldn't bring myself to wear the tattered thing. I was miserable the rest of the evening as I mingled with guests.

Mom's unkind remarks and stinging criticisms escalated. She complained about my weight, the way I ran my home, my family, friends, and how I spent too much time helping "no good people" when I should be helping her more. She said I was a "pious hypocrite."

I turned to the Lord one afternoon in utter anguish: *"God - I can't take anymore. How can I ever gain her approval? No matter what I do—it's never enough."*

I sensed the Lord's gentle voice: *"Carol, Carol...you don't need her approval. You have mine."*

His words calmed my spirit. I might never be able to please my mom, but He approved of me. He then reminded me of an exercise to deal with my problem.

Mentally, I was to take each painful memory as it surfaced, and place it into a yellow backpack. As incident after incident came to mind, I stuffed hurtful words, sad memories, and disappointments into the pack. I pictured the pain filled backpack getting fatter and fatter.

Next, I nailed the bulky pack to the cross where I watched it slowly turn red with the cleansing blood of Jesus. Only then, was I able to let go and forgive. I prayed: *"Oh Lord, as you have forgiven my sins, help me to forgive my mother. Let your love flow through me to her. Help me to let go of all bitterness and resentment."*

In prayer, I saw myself as a young child in the hospital. A young woman was sitting next to my hospital bed, crying and praying for my recovery. It was my mother. With that picture, I knew that deep down she must love me. Jesus counseled me to *"Honor your mother. Treat her the way that you would like her to be."*

I also had to let go of unrealistic expectations of my mother; expectations that only set me up for disappointment. She might never change, but with God's help, I could change.

I took care to find special greeting cards—ones that offered a blessing. I often brought flowers for no special reason. I stopped looking for affirmation from her for my good deeds. Once when she made a crack about our "beach place" I wrote her a letter telling her how much joy it gave me to share my home and blessings with her and Dad. I invited Mom to Aglow meetings with me and took her shopping on occasion. Mom slowly responded to my change in attitude, but more importantly I was shedding much of the bitterness that held me in bondage for so long. I began to see that Mom had a lot of insecurities; and was unsure of herself in many ways. She began asking questions about the Bible and the other books I gave her. Mom and Dad occasionally accompanied us to church, but they seemed uncomfortable in the formal church setting. Instead, they began watching Christian television programs on Sunday mornings.

* * * *

I decided to attend college classes in medical assisting. Ted's travels increased to a frenzied pace. He visited Japan, the Philippines, Indonesia, China, Europe, South America, Africa, and the Caribbean. He would return exhausted, recoup for a few days, and be on the road again. Ryan, now a teenager, kept busy with football games and band concerts. He acted in community theater, and was chosen *Student of the Month* at school. Our recreation room was usually filled with his friends making music, playing whiffle ball in the yard after dark, and swimming in the canal in the summertime. Like most teenagers they ate pizza, ice-cream, hot-dogs, and whatever they could find in the kitchen. Ryan was easy going and a scholar as well.

After completing my college course work, I began working part time.

* * * *

Healing Tears

Both of my parents had escalating health problems. Mom's doctor advised her repeatedly to stop smoking and drinking as her liver was now diseased from a previous blood transfusion. She didn't heed his advice and eventually suffered a stroke. The stroke left her confused and unable to control her bodily functions. She forgot lighted cigarettes and burned holes in her clothing and the furniture. She left pans on burners—starting more than one kitchen fire. She lost track of what was in the fridge and served spoiled food. We had senior meals delivered, but Dad sent them away saying the food was "awful." Mom was unsteady on her feet, and I feared she might tumble down the steps on her way to the washer and dryer in the basement.

Their house was a shambles as Mom watched cartoons and shopping channels on TV most of the day. Her fascination with TV shopping led to outrageous credit card debt. Dad was furious and had to cancel his credit cards. My sister and I tried to help keep their house in order, but the job was too much. We hired a cleaning lady, who did a great job, but Dad told her not to return. He didn't want strangers poking around the house. Nor would he consider outside health care providers. Mom and Dad insisted the family should care for them. Sherry and I tried in vain to reason with them. Dad wasn't well himself and he was overwhelmed. His frustration caused him to lash out at me or anyone else who crossed his path. I was particularly devastated when he cussed me out for asking a simple question. This problem was too big for me to handle. I felt terribly guilty at not being able to solve my parents' problems and angry that they would not consider reasonable solutions we came up with.

* * * *

I decided to take the classes on co-dependency that my friend, Judy, was teaching from a Christian perspective. Her classes helped me discover healthier ways of relating to people. I learned not to enable bad behavior by giving in to unreasonable demands, or doing things for people they should be doing for themselves. In these classes I realized that I was dealing with far more than just a difficult personality with my mother. Her past threats of suicide and emotional abuse were not *normal*. Nor was it normal to be manipulated by guilt.

I learned that it wasn't necessarily my responsibility to rescue everyone who needed a home. Looking back, I counted seventeen people who had resided in my home for an extended period of time. Children are often assigned roles by their parents; mine was that of rescuer/caretaker. I first became a rescuer as a toddler when I tried to stop my father from hitting my mother. I'd been given the task of baby-sitting at an early age. I felt responsible for my brother, Chuckie, when he got into trouble as a kid. Mom once told me the reason he had so many problems was because she spent too much time with me when I was little.

Through these classes I learned to ask myself some key questions when presented with someone's demands:

- Is this the Lord's calling for my life? (Am I really called to take care of Aunt Sarah, or is it my cousin's responsibility to find proper care for her?)
- Is this what I *want* to do, or what someone else expects of me? (Is this a role assigned to me by someone else?)
- Is this my responsibility or not? (Am I responsible for giving my parents 24 hour care? Especially when they don't cooperate.)
- Am I trying to please someone or win their approval?
- Am I responsible for the way people react to my decisions? (If someone chooses to rant and rave, and carry on, so be it. I refuse to be manipulated by their reaction.)

I learned when pressured into an action it's easy to become resentful.

I discovered that it's okay to follow my dreams and goals as the Lord leads. He gives us the desires of our heart as we trust in Him.

I grappled with these insights as I tried setting boundaries with my parents. I was not comfortable standing up to them. It was a stretch. But the next time Dad lashed out in anger, I calmly let him know that his frustration didn't give him the right to attack me verbally. He was surprisingly receptive, and seemed to respect me more for taking a stand. As I learned to set priorities—like asking Mom not to smoke in our home, I no longer suffered in silence. She was welcome to smoke on our covered porch if she liked. She adjusted better than I thought she would. As I had more self respect, Mom seemed to respect me more too. However, a lifetime of reacting is hard to leave behind.

I wrestled with my priorities as I battled ongoing migraine headaches. A friend suggested I meet with a prayer counselor at a local church.

I sat next to a gentle woman and shared some of my concerns. We spent time in prayer asking the Lord to guide our session. The lady instructed me to pray with my eyes closed.

I pictured myself standing at one end of a very large room. A crowd of my relatives and ancestors were gathered at the opposite end of the room. There was a long rope **connecting** us, tying us together.

Jesus was standing in the middle of the room. I asked Him, "What is the rope?"

He answered: *"Infirmity."*

I recalled stories of my grandmother's raging fevers and sleep walking at night. Mom had a goiter surgically removed as a child. She'd been ailing as long as I could remember. I'd struggled with sickness since I was a baby. Gigi had been chronically ill as a child. It all made sense.

We prayed that Jesus would sever the connecting tie. I pictured Him cutting the link with a huge sword. As I spiritually walked through this exercise, something significant occurred. Heaviness lifted from my chest, like when a dental hygienist removes a lead apron after an x-ray.

I've been remarkably healthy since then with a dramatic change in my well-being. The painful migraines are a thing of the past.

* * * *

Meanwhile, things were getting worse for my parents. Mom began falling and Dad telephoned at all hours of the night asking for help getting her off of the floor. The strain was too much for him, he was sick and exhausted. He learned that he had a serious blood disorder requiring frequent transfusions.

We finally convinced them to try an assisted living apartment where their meals were served in a lovely dining hall. Their apartment faced the water and there was a little patio. There was a pull cord in the bedroom and bathroom to summons help if needed. With maid service, and medications delivered by a nurse, things smoothed out considerably. Mom became quite docile— no longer argumentative. She was more loving and no longer seemed to resent me. However, she continued to fall down and before long, a broken hip forced her into a nursing home. Subsequently, she was diagnosed with Parkinson's disease which explained her frequent falls.

Dad's blood disorder was taking its toll on him. The once robust man was rapidly losing weight and stamina. He made an effort to visit Mom every day.

The rest of the time he moped in his apartment complaining about how much it was costing him.

Dad gladly accepted Gigi and Greg's invitation to live with their family. It was stipulated that as long as he was mobile he could stay. He insisted upon paying his own way. One of Gigi's three boys was usually in Dad's lap. These final months were a time of preparation and drawing near to the Lord. He was receptive to ministry and welcomed our prayers. He seemed more at peace than I'd ever known him to be. As his health deteriorated he got his affairs in order.

Over the next few months I juggled my time between working full time at a medical clinic, visiting Mom in the nursing home, and ministering to Dad in the hospital. Ryan was away at college.

My brother, Paul, made frequent trips from California to visit our parents. I got to know him better as he spent time in my home and we opened up with each other. Chuck came too. My sister and I grew closer too as we shared the responsibilities for our folks. We agreed that Sherry would concentrate on meeting Mom's needs while I took care of Dad's.

On Christmas morning we took Mom to visit Dad in the hospital. He was getting a transfusion. His blue eyes lit up when he saw us wheel her into his room.

January was touch-and-go as Dad entered a nursing home. Though he protested we decided to give him a party for his upcoming birthday. I made restaurant reservations and invited the relatives. We ordered a large cake, balloon bouquets, and a giant greeting card—big enough to stand alone on the floor. Everyone wrote a message to Grandpa.

Dad's frail frame seemed to disappear into his blue sweater. An oxygen tank hugged the back of his wheelchair and a clear tube ran from the tank to Dad's nose.

My sister wheeled Mom into the restaurant and parked her chair next to Dad's. His blue eyes sought hers as he reached for her withered hand. Mom smiled and leaned towards him for a kiss. They both ordered lobster, a change in fare from nursing home food. "It tastes real good!" Dad said.

He read his card, and clapped when the waiter brought his cake ablaze with 84 candles. We joined the restaurant staff as they sang *"Happy Birthday."* Great-grandson, Ian, helped blow out the candles. By the time Dad finished his cake he was exhausted. Mercifully, he hadn't choked throughout the entire evening. It had been a wonderful party. Six days later Dad died.

Mom held unrealistic expectations that she and my father would recover and live together again. It broke my heart to tell her that he had passed away. When my sister broke the news she didn't take it well. After his funeral Mom's sad eyes reflected sorrow as she pined away for her mate of 59 years. The only memories she had of him now were good ones. I visited as often as possible, usually bringing flowers. I read to Mom from her favorite book of poems. Sometimes she surprised me by reciting along with me from memory. She'd beg me to stay longer and to take her home with me. But I couldn't possibly give her the kind of care that she was receiving. At Christmas time we decorated her room and brought a small tree. I had plenty of opportunity to share the love of Jesus and to pray with her.

I brought my favorite painting of Jesus smiling at a bird perched on his outstretched finger. I hung it on the wall where Mom could see it at all times.

One afternoon I wheeled Mom back from her cigarette break. She was smiling with a far away look of love and tenderness in her eyes.

"What are you thinking, Mom?"

She surprised me by answering softly: "I'm just sitting here, loving you."

"I love you too, Mom." *God truly does give us the desires of our heart.* My heart mended that afternoon as we embraced.

One evening I tiptoed into Mom's room and studied her as she slept peacefully. Her gray hair was tied at the nape of her neck with a black ribbon. I kissed her forehead and she opened her eyes. "Carol...." She smiled and grasped my hand.

"Hi, Mom. How are you feeling?"

"Okay, dear, how are you?"

"I'm fine."

"I missed you." *My mother had missed me, my mother loved me. Thank you, Jesus.* "I missed you too Mom."

My Mother died in early spring. After her memorial service I went to the nursing home to get the last of her things. As I gave the picture of Jesus to Mom's roommate, I took one last look at His face. His eyes mirrored compassion and unfailing love.

Unfailing love. That says it so perfectly. Jesus has always been and still is my source of unfailing love. He has forgiven my sins, redeemed my troubled past and healed my wounds. Unfailing Love is the anchor that keeps me from crashing on the rocks during the storms of life. It's a love that will never, never let me go for all eternity.

The End....is yet to be.....

Printed in the United States
20278LVS00001B/160-405

9 781594 671401